T0151250

silk road vegetarian

Vegan, Vegetarian *and* Gluten Free Recipes *for the* Mindful Cook

DAHLIA ABRAHAM-KLEIN

TUTTLE Publishing

Tokyo | Rutland, Vermont | Singapore

Contents

8 **Foreword**

10 **Introduction**

20 **The Spice Pantry**

26 **Basic Preparation**

(V = Vegan; GF = Gluten Free; DF = Dairy Free)

Bases, Condiments & Other Useful Recipes

41 Hummus Dip V GF

42 Sesame Seed Paste V GF

42 Tomato Paste V GF

43 North African Chili Paste V GF

43 Raita GF

44 Oven Roasted Nuts

44 Toasted Seeds and Spices

44 Za'atar Spice Mix

45 Vegetable Broth V GF

46 Shawarma Spice Mix

46 Applesauce

47 Tahini Sauce V GF

47 Duck Sauce V GF

48 Mango Chutney V GF

48 Tofu Mayonnaise V GF

49 Coconut Milk V GF

Appetizers

52 Bukharian Vegan Chopped Liver V GF

54 Chickpea Falafel V GF

55 Mediterranean Chickpea Salad V GF

56 Stuffed Grape Leaves V GF

58 Persian Green Frittata GF DF

60 Turkish Leek Patties GF DF

61 Persian Cucumber Yogurt Dip GF

62 Persian Spinach & Yogurt Dip GF

63 Italian Zucchini Fritters GF

64 Indian Red Lentil Falafel V GF

65 Roasted Eggplant Paté V GF

Soups

68 Lentil Tomato Soup V GF

70 Persian Bean & Noodle Soup V GF

72 Pumpkin Soup V GF

73 Lentil & Carrot Soup V GF

74 Split Pea Soup V GF

75 Gingered Sweet Potato Soup V GF

76 Sweet Potato & Lentil Soup V GF

77 Spiced Red Lentil Soup V GF

78 Yellow Split Pea Soup V GF

80 Butternut Squash Soup V GF

81 Curried Parsnip Soup V GF

Salads

84 Sesame Kale Salad V GF

85 Asian Coleslaw V GF

86 Orange & Fennel Salad V GF

87 Minted Beet Salad GF

88 Crunchy Broccoli Salad GF

89 Mushrooms with Cumin V GF

90 Curried Spinach Salad with Apples & Grapes V GF

91 Roasted Cauliflower Salad V GF

92 Middle Eastern Lemon Potato Salad V GF

94 Raw Beet Salad in Lime Vinaigrette V GF

94 Carrot Salad with Garlic & Lemon V GF

95 Red Cabbage Slaw with Tahini Dressing V GF

95 Bukharian Tomato Salad V GF

96 Quinoa Salad with Parsley & Tomatoes V GF

97 Roasted Carrots with Feta & Parsley GF

98 Israeli Chopped Salad V GF

99 Roasted Beet & Nectarine Salad V GF

Main Dishes

102 Persian Eggplant Stew V GF
104 Sweet-Savory Chickpea Curry V GF
105 Afghan Squash Goulash V GF
106 Simmered Red Lentils with Vegetables V GF
107 Red Lentil Curry V GF
108 Indian Spinach Curry V GF
109 Mushroom Curry V GF
110 Curried Lentil Burgers GF DF
111 Chickpea Dal in Coconut Broth V GF
112 Persian Yellow Split Pea Stew V GF
114 Stuffed Acorn Squash with Cinnamon-Spiced Apples & Raisins V GF
116 Bengali Potato & Zucchini Curry V GF
117 Afghan Eggplant Moussaka with Garlic Yogurt Sauce GF
118 Afghan Cauliflower Curry V GF
119 Stuffed Peppers V GF
120 Turkish Baked Eggplant with Mint V GF
122 Bukharian Stuffed Cabbage V GF
124 Bukharian Stuffed Onions V GF
126 Persian Green-Herbed Stew V GF

Rice Dishes

130 Bukharian Mung Bean Rice with Garlic Oil V GF
132 Swiss Chard Pilaf V GF
133 Simple Steamed Brown Rice
133 Boiled Rice
134 Bukharian Green-Herbed Rice V GF
135 Syrian Lentils & Rice V GF
136 Steamed Rice with Egg & Saffron Crust GF DF
138 Fragrant Indian Pilaf V GF
139 Spanakorizo GF
140 Afghan Risotto V GF
142 Bukharian Pilaf with Kidney Beans & Carrots V GF
144 Bukharian Slow-Cooked Rice with Dried Fruit V GF
145 Mushroom Wild Rice V GF
146 Persian Lentil Rice V GF
148 Bukharian Garlic & Chickpea Rice V GF
150 Persian Dill Rice V GF
152 Persian Orange Peel Rice V GF

Side Dishes

156 Zucchini with Basil Vinaigrette V GF
157 Sesame Noodles V GF
158 Casablanca Quinoa V GF
159 Spinach Stuffed Portobello Mushrooms GF
160 Cinnamon-Spiced Butternut Rings V GF
160 Maple-Mustard Roasted Parsnips V GF
161 Roasted Sweet Potatoes with Coriander Chutney V GF
162 Lemony Roasted Vegetables V GF
163 Okra Curry V GF
163 Rutabaga Oven Fries V GF
164 Shawarma-Spiced Potato Wedges V GF
165 Curried Green Beans V GF

Desserts

168 Hamentashen Cookies V GF
170 Baked Lemon Rice Pudding V GF
171 Peach Cobbler V GF
171 Halvah Parfait V GF
172 Persian Rice Cookies GF DF
173 Rhubarb Crisp V GF
174 Zucchini Loaf V GF
175 Spiced Clove Plum Cake V GF
176 Rice-Flour Malabi V GF
177 Orange Blossom Date Balls V GF
178 Cardamom Banana Bread V GF
179 Spiced Carrot Cake V GF
180 Orange Zest Almond Cookies V GF
181 South African Crunchies V GF
182 Berry-Almond Coconut Scones V GF
183 Indian Spiced Coconut Cardamom Tapioca V GF
184 Cinnamon-Apple Cake V GF
185 Indian Rice Pudding V GF

186 **Acknowledgments**
187 **Resources of Interest**
188 **Index**

Published by Tuttle Publishing, an imprint of
Periplus Editions (HK) Ltd.

www.tuttlepublishing.com

Copyright © 2014 Dahlia Abraham-Klein

All rights reserved. No part of this publication may be
reproduced or utilized in any form or by any means, electronic
or mechanical, including photocopying, recording, or by
any information storage and retrieval system, without prior
written permission from the publisher.

Library of Congress Cataloging-in-Publication Data

Abraham-Klein, Dahlia.
 Silk Road vegetarian : vegan, vegetarian and gluten free
recipes for the mindful cook / Dahlia Abraham-Klein ;
foreword by Stephanie Weaver. -- First edition.
     192 pages : color illustrations ; 23 cm
  ISBN 978-0-8048-4337-9 (pbk.)
 1. Vegetarian cooking--Asia. 2. Silk Road. I. Title.
  TX837.A258 2014
  641.5'636095--dc23
                              2013040337

ISBN 978-0-8048-4337-9

Distributed by
North America, Latin America & Europe
Tuttle Publishing
364 Innovation Drive
North Clarendon, VT 05759-9436 U.S.A.
Tel: (802) 773-8930; Fax: (802) 773-6993
info@tuttlepublishing.com
www.tuttlepublishing.com

Japan
Tuttle Publishing
Yaekari Building, 3rd Floor
5-4-12 Osaki, Shinagawa-ku
Tokyo 141 0032
Tel: (81) 3 5437-0171; Fax: (81) 3 5437-0755
sales@tuttle.co.jp
www.tuttle.co.jp

Asia Pacific
Berkeley Books Pte. Ltd.
3 Kallang Sector #04-01
Singapore 349278
Tel: (65) 6741 2178; Fax: (65) 6741 2179
inquiries@periplus.com.sg
www.tuttlepublishing.com

First edition
25 24 23 22 21
10 9 8 7 6 5 4

Printed in Malaysia   2105VP

TUTTLE PUBLISHING® is a registered trademark of
Tuttle Publishing, a division of Periplus Editions (HK) Ltd.

**A portion of the author's proceeds will go to hunger
relief organizations in the U.S. and around the world.**

Photo Credits

Front cover and pages 7, 50, 53, 58, 64, 69, 71, 82, 84, 85, 88, 93, 99, and 108: **Jennifer Jagusak**

Back cover flap and page 14 (author photos): **Daniella Abraham**

The Ultimate Food Journey

Foreword by **Stephanie Weaver**

Silk Road. Have two words ever carried more exotic intrigue? Dahlia Abraham-Klein takes us on a culinary journey through the lands of her heritage. While reading the book I learned about her family, I sat at her table, I tasted her food.

Dahlia traces her family's history back to the Babylonian Exile of the Jewish people during the sixth century BCE. Her ancestors have lived in present day Iraq, Uzbekistan, Afghanistan, Pakistan and India. More recently her parents traveled the world and her mother incorporated all the cuisines she tasted into dishes that melded with their Central-Asian Jewish heritage. Dahlia's recipes emphasize the use of spices, legumes, and grains. She offers in-depth information on these staples we take for granted, improving our cooking and allowing us to savor the flavors even more deeply.

What makes this book unique is that it is vegetarian, making it supremely accessible to so many readers. You can serve these dishes alongside meat or—as I do—make them the flavorful centerpieces of a plant-based table. Dahlia and I have a similar story, finding wellness and healing through changing our diets by eliminating wheat, dairy, meat, and sugar. As a plant-based cook and blogger, I appreciate that this book is filled with recipes I can make without having to make substitutions. Gluten-free recipes are clearly labeled, and the book brims with a healthful ethos. At the same time, all readers will feel welcome at her table, no matter their dietary preferences.

I treasure cookbooks that take me on a journey, that challenge me to incorporate a palette of spices with vegetables and use them successfully. I had never stuffed

"I treasure cookbooks that take me on a journey, that challenge me to incorporate a palette of spices with vegetables and use them successfully."

grape leaves or made falafel before; now I have. The falafels, made with red lentils instead of chickpeas, were light, fluffy, and crispy. The grape leaves had deep, complex flavors with a tangy zing, unlike any grape leaves I have ever eaten before. As I leaf through these pages I can practically smell the savory soups, taste the crisp salads, and I begin to envision dinner parties revolving around the various main, side, and rice dishes. I'm looking forward to following a sumptuous vegetarian meal with the Baked Lemon Rice Pudding or the tasty Rhubarb Crisp.

I love the array of spices that Dahlia skillfully blends, and the rich historical context that she relates through these recipes. I know that she and her family have made them time and again. Her authority shines through on page after beautiful page. Having started a communi-ty-supported agriculture group in her Long Island community, Dahlia is in tune with seasonal eating. The realities of urban life in the cool Northeast, however, have led her to become an expert at freezing fruits and vegetables at their peak to enjoy later. I appreciated the step-by-step instructions explaining how and why to use different techniques to make the most of my freezer.

Savor this book, read the introduction and early chapters, understand how and why these recipes came to be. And then, say grace and enjoy.

Stephanie Weaver
author of the Recipe Renovator blog and
Golden Angels: A Pet Loss Memoir

My Culinary Pilgrimage

Every Wednesday, I anxiously check my watch every few minutes until 2 p.m., the hour I pull my car out of the garage to make room for the load of fresh veggies for my Community Supported Agriculture group. At the stroke of two, Cornelius, the driver from Golden Earthworm, a farm on the east end of Long Island, New York, skillfully maneuvers his refrigerated truck just below the drive. He and Edvin, the farmer, are already exhausted from a long day's work, but they haul box after box up the steep incline to my garage.

Slowly, the garage blossoms—until every nook and cranny holds a box near bursting with good, organically grown foods, the scent of earth still clinging to the just-picked produce. Soon, the CSA will open its doors and the members will come to collect their weekly boxes, buzzing with excitement to see what's inside. For a few minutes, though, I'm alone with the bounty of summer, fragrant and ready to eat—ears of silken sweet corn, fragrant summer peaches, ripe red tomatoes, sleek green zucchini, dimpled raspberries the color of jewels.

I've traveled a long journey to arrive in the middle of this cornucopia. And though it might sound odd, it was a journey that began before I was born—several centuries before, actually, when my ancestors headed east from ancient Israel to Central Asia, joining countless other travelers on the storied trade route known as the Silk Road, where both commodities and cultures mingled. Sometimes, when I'm cozily ensconced in my home in Long Island, New York, surrounded by the riches of my CSA, I feel as though I am traveling with them, still on a Silk Road of sorts. My parents, Yehuda and Zina, instilled in me a love of learning about the many cultures of the world, and this love was often manifest at our table. Like so many people who love food and its historical aspects, I pick up recipes and ideas everywhere I go, from almost everyone I meet, and I fold them into my kitchen repertoire, just as my ancestors did.

But I'm getting ahead of myself. I grew up in New York, in a home where fresh, home-cooked food and enthusiastic entertaining, whether with our large extended family or international business associates, was the norm rather than the exception. Our dinner table regularly sat twenty guests from all over the world and was often elbow-to-elbow full. During the holidays, my parents adopted the literal meaning of the biblical words, "All who are hungry, let them come and eat." It was a festive tableau of silverware clanking, wine goblets clinking to the words, "*L'chaim*—To life," a table overflowing with luscious heirloom rice dishes and stuffed vegetables, aromatic stews and fresh fruits.

What distinguished my parents from those of my classmates was that they were part of the ancient Jewish community of Central Asia. In modern times, our family members were scattered all over the world, in Italy, Israel, Thailand, Hong Kong, Japan, and the U.S., but they could all trace their ancestry to the Babylonian Exile and Persian conquest, in the sixth century BCE. At that time, the great Temple in Jerusalem was destroyed and the Jews were forced into exile in Babylonia (now Iraq), which, in turn, was conquered by Persia (now Iran). For several centuries, my family traveled between Persia, Afghanistan and Bukhara (the capital of a province in Uzbekistan) as merchants; they spoke their own Jewish dialect of Farsi, Judeo-Persian, and cooked a kosher interpretation of the local food. In the

My paternal great grandfather near the Pyramids in 1914.

A family wedding party in Kabul in 1940.

ABOVE LEFT: My father at a 1960s Passover Seder meal wearing a traditional silk brocade called a *jomah*. He is holding a green onion as an illustration for one of the songs.
ABOVE CENTER: My grandfather buying sapphires in Burma in the 1960s.

early part of the nineteenth century, my family finally settled down in Afghanistan, smack in the middle of the Silk Road.

THE SILK ROAD'S CULINARY HERITAGE

For those in the West familiar with it, most equate the Silk Road with China and its immediate neighbors, when in fact it was an extensive, interconnected network of trade routes across the Asian continent connecting East, South, and West Asia with the Mediterranean world, culminating in Italy. These Silk Routes (collectively known as the Silk Road) were important paths for cultural and commercial exchange between traders, merchants, pilgrims, missionaries, soldiers, and nomads from China, India, Tibet, the Persian Empire, and Mediterranean countries for almost 3,000 years.

The lucrative Chinese silk trade, which began during the Han Dynasty (206 BCE–220 CE) gave the "road" its name. Silk, however, was hardly the only commodity that moved along the route. All sorts of goods were traded—chief among them, spices, which were prized for their culinary, medicinal, and cosmetic value.

It's the culinary heritage of the Silk Road that most fascinates me. If you could visualize the foods of the Silk Road, you'd see a collection of interconnecting sweeps and swirls revealing similarities and variations among cuisines and cultures. Reflecting the influence of the silk and spice trades, there are tastes of India and China in all the cuisines found along the Silk Road; above all, though, the Silk Road is a rich mosaic—each piece related but distinctly different. The same basic dish may be prepared in several different regions, but will vary depending on what grows in each place, how the local people expressed their nationalism, religion, and culture in their cooking, and how they were influenced by travelers. Many Central Asians, my family included, were a motley crew weaving through the trade routes and picking up their customs and dishes along their travels.

ABOVE: My sister, being held by my father, at her first birthday party in Bombay.

Most of the dishes of the region made use of local vegetables and the fundamental staple of the Silk Road: rice. The grain was first cultivated in China and India, and it was at least 5,000 years before it reached Persia in the fourth century BCE. Rice did not play an important role until the eighth century CE, but after that it became the centerpiece of the festive dishes called *polows*, known under different spellings in neighboring countries. The Bukharian green rice dish known as *baksh* is a variation on the Persian *shevid polo,* while the Bukharian *oshi mosh* (which looks just like it sounds) is a variation of the Indian *kitchari*, which is a staple comfort food in that country.

MY FAMILY'S CULINARY HERITAGE IN CENTRAL ASIA

My paternal great grandfather, known as Amin Kabuli, owned a vinyard in the region that is known today as Samarkand, Uzbekistan. The grapes were transformed into preserves and also wine, which was used locally for the Sabbath or sold for export. In fact, the Rothschild family heard about his renowned wine, and came to Samarkand requesting the seeds of his gigantic jeweled grapes so they could plant them in a vineyard in Israel. (When my paternal grandmother moved to the United States in the 1950s, she continued her family's ancient tradition of growing grapes and making her own wine. My parents still have wine that she made over 40 years ago.)

In my grandfather's day, Bukhara was a city in a southern province of Russia. As toddlers, my parents moved with their respective families to Kabul. There, my mother and her six siblings lived in a Jewish quarter, in an inner courtyard with closed gates, along with other families. The kitchen was a communal kitchen, of sorts. In the courtyard was a makeshift clay oven known as a *tandoor* that everyone used. The women in the courtyard would occasionally meet, serving tea along with a little gossip, a few jokes, and lots of laughter. To add to the congestion, many families kept a lamb and raised chickens in the courtyard to be ritually slaughtered for festive occasions. Large families and communal living demanded a practical solution to the challenge of meal preparation. Silk Road cooks found inspiration in one-pot meals consisting of all the essential ingredients for a balanced diet— not just in Afghanistan, but in Iran and Uzbekistan as well.

Most Westerners think of meat kabobs when they think of Persian and Afghan fare, but in truth, families rarely ate meat at home; it was saved for celebrations and holidays. Thus, Silk Road cooking had a strong vegetarian focus, partly due to the various religions flourishing there that encouraged a vegetarian diet, but chiefly because of economics. Vegetarian food was simply more affordable than meat.

As a result, preserving foods was essential in order to extend the season for all the fruits and vegetables that came to the table. Nearly every home had a big cellar for preserves, while root vegetables were kept covered with earth to preserve their freshness. Nothing went to waste—no composting was necessary, because all kitchen scraps were used as soup bases and fruit scraps were turned into preserves.

Despite the difficulties, a spirit of abundance shone throughout the cuisine. With rice, vegetables, fruit, nuts, and plenty of spices used in combination, there was always plenty to eat.

**LEFT: My mother (third from the left) scooping out a *pilou* in the 1960s.
BELOW: Berry-Almond Coconut Scones (page 182) fresh from the oven.**

MY FAMILY'S CULINARY HERITAGE IN INDIA

My mother lived in Kabul until she was a teenager, and then moved to Israel in 1949, a year after its founding. My father grew up in Kabul and worked as a tradesman before moving to Peshawar in what would become, when the British granted it independence, Pakistan. In 1947, the war between Pakistan and India prompted my father to move to Bombay, where he remained until he was thirty years old. During that time he visited Israel; he met my mother there, and they married in 1952. India was their home until 1956.

Bombay (now Mumbai) had been another stop for the traders and travelers of the Silk Road, and by the time my parents got there it was a melting pot of cultures, all drawn by the economic potential of this vibrant city. It was only natural that Bombay's cuisine was as diverse as the country itself; however, there were certain characteristics that were unique to India. Because India was a predominantly Hindu country with a strong respect for life, many people followed the Hindu practice of strict vegetarianism. My newlywed mother quickly incorporated the Indian gastronomy, learning and cooking even more vegetarian dishes, which were prepared with cardamom, cinnamon, cumin, ginger, and mustard seed, to name just a few of the spices in her cabinet.

It was common for Jewish families like mine, with roots on the Silk Road, to trade as merchants. From their headquarters in Kabul, my family operated a diverse business that included the colorful world of gemstones, fabrics, and garments, as well as commodities such as car parts and tires. The business involved intercontinental transactions, so it was necessary to establish offices around the globe. My uncles opened satellite offices in Tokyo, Kobe, Hong Kong, Bombay, Bangkok, Milan, Valencia, Tel Aviv, and Chiasso and Lugano, in Switzerland. At the same time my parents headed for New York, and often traveled to the various world capitals.

MY OWN CULINARY TALE

Because of my father's work and my family's frequent travels, my parents absorbed the cultures, languages, tastes, and cuisines of all the places they lived in. They often entertained my father's business associates, and my mother's role as matriarch was to host and cook meals that made our guests feel at home. Our live-in helpers also came from diverse cultures and contributed their own favorites to our table. All these experiences influenced our cultural repertoire and expanded our culinary curiosity. The food I grew up with was an intermarriage of exotic tastes from Asian, African, European, Indian, and even some Latin dishes that formed a harmonious and tasty bliss. We were all always learning and sharing our cultures through cuisine.

What was unusual and wonderful about my mother's cooking was that she was inspired by every culture she encountered and she instinctively knew how to integrate her native mix of Persian, Central Asian, and Indian food into any new cuisine she was learning about. Even before culinary adventurism became popular, she courageously tasted any and every ethnic cuisine she could try, and eventually incorporated them into her own delicious signature dishes.

And so I grew up, a typical New York kid in some ways, and in others a citizen of the world—at least at the table. As an adult, however, I did not follow my mother's example at first. In traveling frequently and leading the lifestyle of a single New Yorker—with little time for home cooking or eating well—I gradually grew chronically ill, debilitated from a painful ulcer. While in New York, my typical diet was a doughnut in the morning, followed by pizza or a sandwich for lunch, and pasta for dinner. When I look back at those years, I'm astonished that I settled for eating so poorly. Back then, my goal was "eat to live," and to do so as quickly as possible. Notice that I was not eating "live" foods, but processed quick-and-easy meals designed just to fill me up.

I went to see a conventional gastroenterologist who feebly attempted to correct my diet, suggesting bland foods like dairy and toast, and discouraging spicy foods. He then sent me off with a handful of medications. He did not ask me what my diet was like or what my heritage was; nor did he bother to investigate whether I had any food sensitivities. After months of following the regimen, I was not feeling any better and I decided to consult a holistic nutritionist. The nutritionist urged me to eliminate all wheat, dairy, and sugar from my diet. Ironically, wheat and dairy are precisely what the gastroenterologist had told me to eat! He also told me that I could eat spicy foods because I had grown up on them—that I should eat in harmony with my ancestral cuisine.

My first thought was, "What am I going to eat if I can't eat wheat, dairy, and sugar?" And yet my body was taxed from years of over-consumption of processed foods. These three ingredients—wheat, dairy, and sugar—were wreaking havoc on my immune system. I plumbed my memories of my mother's table and found answers in my ancestral cuisine.

Reacquainting myself with the diet of my childhood, which consisted largely of rice, vegetables, fruits, and beans, I discovered that the transformation wasn't as difficult as I'd anticipated—especially because I felt so much better! My palate sobered up after many years of being "drugged." I soon began detecting the artificial chemical flavors in processed foods that I'd never noticed before. Another added benefit was that, without the heavy carbohydrates and sugar fogging up my mind, my thinking became sharper. And I found that cooking engaged my spirit. Making healthy choices in the foods I ate was truly liberating.

Inspired to learn more about the link between food and wellness, I studied natural health and subsequently opened my own practice as a naturopath in 1994. In the ensuing years, I helped patients with chronic health issues—many related to food sensitivities. As a frequent guest on the *Gary Null Radio Show*, I addressed the concerns of listeners struggling with the same problems I once faced.

MY CULINARY CONVERSION

I'd been veering toward vegetarianism shortly after my second marriage to my South African husband. Mervin was already accustomed to healthy eating, purchasing food from the local food co-op and preparing homemade South African vegetarian meals. South Africa is a melting pot of cuisines, thanks to several waves of massive immigration, particularly Indian.

Gastronomically speaking, we create an interesting Central Asian-African blend.

The turning point in our commitment to meat abstinence was shortly after we adopted Flynn, a sweet-natured cocker spaniel with an uncannily human face and a sweet, honest spirit. Abused by previous owners who cruelly dumped him onto the streets of Manhattan, Flynn was terribly skittish. He needed my full attention and pampering to recover from his ordeal.

On one particular Sabbath, my son, husband, and I, with Flynn by our side, sat at the table. Mervin recited the blessing over the wine and bread. That night I served garlic-rosemary roasted chicken. As I gazed at the headless chicken on my table, I looked over at Flynn's gentle face, and I was struck by an epiphany. I realized that his presence in my life had altered my way of thinking. I questioned whether I could live with and love this needy animal while remaining a meat-eater. My conscience stung. Why was it okay to kill even one animal when we are all part of nature?

Thinking back, it's no wonder that this thought struck me while we were sitting together over a sacred Sabbath meal, which is carefully chosen and prepared to remind us that we are not alone in the world, but are part of a collective wave of conscious thought on how we sow, how we harvest, how we slaughter, and how we eat. My relationship with Flynn taught me that vegetarianism is life-affirming; a vegetarian lifestyle expresses gratitude for our animal kingdom, rather than entitlement and ownership.

As my commitment to healthy and ethical eating grew, it was a natural progression to begin to purchase my foods from a local source. I decided to start a CSA (Community Supported Agriculture) program in my neighborhood. Golden Earthworm Farm became my partner, with some 40 like-minded households. The community connects through the rituals of harvesting, cooking, and sharing. We thrive on the joy of cooking whole foods and breaking bread together.

As time went on, I noticed that, as enthusiastic as they were, many of the CSA members had no idea what to do with some of the produce in their boxes. I was only too happy to share recipes, which culminated in my compiling a seasonal cookbook. *Silk Road Vegetarian* is an outgrowth of that first volume.

LOCAL AND SEASONAL EATING

It's amazing to think that less than fifty years ago, almost all fruits and vegetables throughout the world were locally produced. That meant that people in tropical climates would have eaten tropical fruit in the fall, and people in northern climates would have eaten fruits like apples and pears. Today, most fruits in the supermarket are picked long before they are ripe, and sit in a truck or depot ripening for weeks before they get to us. But there's a cost to this method, and it's paid in quality. Foods that need to be shipped long distances are genetically bred to look presentable even when they're old, rather than bred for taste or nutrition. The longer the produce sits before being eaten, the less its nutritional value to us.

When we purchase from a supermarket, we often don't take into account the distance the produce must travel to reach our plates and the intervention that takes place to keep it in optimum condition. By buying from a farmers' market or becom-

ABOVE: Here I'm wearing a traditional silk Bukharian brocade reserved for special occasions.
ABOVE RIGHT: My husband and I wearing silk *jomahs*.

ing a member of a CSA program—that is, buying a subscription for a season's worth of produce from a local farm—you can be sure that your produce has been picked the same day that it's ripe and delivered that very same day, as well. In this way, we are getting the optimal nutrition from the foods we eat, while minimizing energy consumption and waste involved in transporting foods for great distances.

The notion of buying locally grown produce might seem to be a bit of a conundrum in colder climates, where the growing season is short. However, winter root vegetables, some hothouse-grown foods, and preserved and frozen produce can be substituted for fresh.

As we understand and respond to the relationship between planet and plate, we can regain the balance in our lives and on our planet, reawaken our taste buds, and leave the world a better place for future generations.

AND SO, A BOOK

These recipes are inspired by my mother's Silk Road cookery, and all the ingenious, loving Silk Road cooks who came before her. In my imagination, I've extended Silk Road cuisine all the way to Long Island, as I make use of local ingredients and combine them with seeds, pods, spices, and everything in-between to mimic the essence and flavor of the trade route. And in the same way that Central Asian food was adapted to varying tastes and lifestyles along the Silk Road, I have adapted my recipes to our modern American techniques and sensibilities.

My recipes also reflect my own preference for vegetarian fare that is free of wheat, gluten, and dairy. (Each recipe is labeled to identify its vegan, dairy-free, and gluten-free status.) I've tried to make the dishes appealing to all, whether strict or "occasional" vegetarians. For meat eaters who experience vegetarian meals as

Unloading another fresh delivery from Golden Earthworm Farm on the east end of Long Island, New York.

CSA member pick up.

lacking fullness, Silk Road-style spices can add a whole new dimension to your food.

I have heard some complain that a vegetarian diet is too time consuming and labor intensive for our modern world. It's true that this food requires a good bit of peeling and chopping. Remember, though, that a good and healthy vegetarian diet isn't supposed to be eaten in a car or on the run. Enjoying flavors and food, whether in the presence of those you care for or on your own, is good for your soul—your spirit will sit up and take notice.

Because I'm not a trained chef and have no formal culinary education, I have been very conscientious in creating a recipe book that is easy to follow. If I can cook these dishes, anyone can! Regardless of previous experience in the kitchen, these recipes are accessible to the home cook. While some require more practice and skill, most are suitable for the novice.

By both personal inclination and the tenets of my religion, I passionately believe we must all be good stewards of our planet. I've designed my recipes to foster seasonal eating. To this end, I've also included a section on food preservation through freezing (page 35) for readers whose local farms don't have a year-round growing season. In this way, when you have an abundant supply of produce, you can preserve it when fresh and use it when it's not in season.

Sharing my dishes with you is a sacred experience for me and I share them with love, from my heart and my hands, in the hope that when we cook together, we can create a groundswell of well-being for all. It is at the table that we connect with one another, our animals, our land, and our past. Cook, eat and enjoy!

www.silkroadvegetarian.com

The Spice Pantry

The exotic scent of spices—rich, alluring and almost magical. Fragrances that infuse the air with an enthralling bouquet. That is what spices do to me—transport me to a dreamy and transcendental place. But spices do more than add flavor and interest to ordinary ingredients. They were a vital commodity on the Silk Road.

Spices are used liberally throughout the recipes in this cookbook. They are my friends, each one having a very specific color, texture and flavor—always adding excitement to any meal while warming the heart. When I was growing up, I never saw my mother use a measuring spoon. This is typical with Old World women, who use their fingers to sprinkle a little of this or throw in a little of that. They cook from a place of passion and intuition, continually adding spices and tasting till the desired state perfection is achieved. Since I started cooking, I have become something of a scientist with spices—experimenting with blending them to attain unique flavors. I encourage you to do the same. Eventually, when you feel confident with your spices, you can decide how much to add of a particular seasoning without measuring. In time, your intuition will guide your senses to play with spices like an artist mixing paint to achieve that ideal color. Brilliant reds, yellows, greens, and a dozen other shades in every imaginable shape, size, and texture sit in my spice rack, mysteriously telling me how to use them. They will talk to you too.

YOUR SPICE PANTRY

I have developed this must-have seasoning and spice pantry for myself and it can be the foundation of your modern Silk Road-inspired cooking, as well.

A FEW THINGS TO REMEMBER

Store dried spices in clean, airtight bottles, in a cool, dark place. Whole spices will keep for a year or two.

Ground spices will lose pungency after four or five months. Aroma is the best indication of freshness. A rule of thumb: little smell, little taste.

Whole spices ground by hand provide the best flavor and aroma. Grind your spices as you need them and do not be tempted to grind too much, as the surplus tends to lose potency and flavor when stored. Some spices, such as cloves, turmeric and cinnamon are difficult to grind at home and are better bought already ground.

Spice grinders come in an assortment of styles, with varying functionality. Some people prefer the look and feel of a mortar and pestle, while others want the efficiency and convenience of a coffee grinder or electric grinder.

ALLSPICE is the dried unripe fruit (actually, the berries) of *Pimenta dioica*, a mid-canopy tree native to the Greater Antilles, Southern Mexico, and Central America, and now cultivated in many warm parts of the world. The English, who thought it combined the flavor of cinnamon, nutmeg and cloves, coined the name "allspice" as early as 1621. Allspice is indispensable in Middle Eastern cuisine, where it is used to flavor a variety of stews. In America and in Great Britain, it is used mostly in desserts, because it has a wonderfully strong aroma that balances sweetness and heat. In Silk Road cookery, it is used in both sweet and savory applications. It does indeed taste like a blend of nutmeg, cinnamon, and cloves. Although allspice is available ready-ground, it is best to buy the spice whole to retain its flavor, and grind just before use.

Medicinally, allspice has been used as a deodorant and has also been said to provide relief for indigestion and gas.

BAY LEAF grows on the coast of the Black and Mediterranean Seas. It refines and adds aroma to many sour dishes and is typically added to soups and stews because of its pungent flavor. Since these leaves are so pungent, one is generally enough for a dish, and the leaf is removed prior to serving the dish. Look for pale, green and unbroken leaves for best flavor. They're usually sold dried.

BLACK PEPPER is native to India and has been a prized spice since ancient times. It was cherished for its ability to add pungency to bland foods, and to disguise a food's lack of freshness when there was no efficient means of preservation available.

Pepper became an important spice that stimulated much of the spice trade, due to its varied uses. Pepper loses flavor and aroma when exposed to the air, so airtight storage helps preserve its original spiciness. Once ground, pepper's aromatics can dissipate quickly, which is why it's best to grind whole peppercorns immediately before use.

CARDAMOM comes from the seeds of a plant that, like ginger, can be propagated through its *rhizomes* (stems that grow mostly underground, in tangled masses). But unlike ginger, it is the seed-pods that find their way into the spice pantry. These can be used whole or split, but either way, must be cooked. You can also bruise (lightly smash) the pod to open it, and fry the seeds before adding the main ingredients to the pan. And you can pound them with other spices to make a blend.

Cardamom has a distinct, warm, sweet, pungent aroma and tastes like a combination of citrus, camphor, and eucalyptus. Toasted, ground, or in its whole form, cardamom's versatility is incredible; it infuses all kinds of dishes with a distinctive flavor note. Curries, breads, desserts, rice, tea, and coffee can all benefit from the addition of cardamom. Bruised green pods have a stronger and sweeter aroma than black cardamom pods that are found in Asia and Australia.

Cardamom loses its flavor and aroma quickly. It's best to purchase it in its whole pod form and grind what you need when you need it. Even the pods will lose up to 40 percent of their potency during their first year in storage.

CINNAMON is native to Sri Lanka. The brown bark of the cinnamon tree, which is available in its dried tubular form known as a quill, or as ground powder. Although

available throughout the year, the fragrant, sweet, and warm taste of cinnamon is a perfect spice to use during the winter months. The two varieties of cinnamon, Chinese and Ceylon, have a similar flavor; however, the cinnamon from Ceylon is slightly sweeter and more refined, with a greater concentration of oils. Which should you use? It depends on what you're cooking—and your budget. Ceylon cinnamon is more difficult to find; you will have to seek it out in specialty spice shops. Cassia, as Chinese cinnamon is known, is more widely available; it's what's usually stocked at your local grocery store. Keep cinnamon in a tightly sealed glass container in a cool, dark, and dry place. The refrigerator will help extend cinnamon's freshness. If it no longer smells sweet, it's stale and should be tossed.

CLOVES have a strong, peculiar aroma and a sweet-hot-spicy flavor. They can

easily overpower a dish, particularly when ground, so only use a dash. They are often used in curry powders, hot drinks with wine, punches, fruit juices, desserts, and stewed fruits.

CORIANDER refers to the seeds and leaves of an annual herb; in the U.S., the leaves are called cilantro and the seeds are called coriander. And in some places, the leaves are known as Chinese parsley.

Whatever you call it; this distinctive herb has a flavor that can be likened to a blend of lemon and sage. All parts of the plant are edible, but it's the fresh leaves and the dried seeds that are commonly used in cooking, and many cultures have made it an integral part of traditional dishes.

CUMIN is an aromatic spice with a distinctive, bitter, earthy flavor with a hint of lemon and a strong, warm aroma due to its high oil content. Cumin "seeds" are actually the small dried fruit of this annual plant, which is a member of the parsley family. Native to the Mediterranean, cumin is sometimes confused with caraway, but it is hotter to the taste, lighter in color, and larger. Sold whole or ground, the seeds come in three colors: amber, white, or black. Amber is most widely available. If you find the black variety, be warned; it has such a complex flavor that it should not be substituted for the other two. Cumin is a popular ingredient in Middle Eastern, Asian, Mediterranean, and Mexican cuisines, and is one of the main ingredients in curry powder. Toasting the seeds enhances their flavor.

CURRY POWDER is a blend of several spices that are ground and mixed in certain proportions. (Every Silk Road cook has a favorite formula; in the West it is typically sold pre-mixed.) It is composed of coriander, turmeric, chilies, cumin, pepper, ginger, cinnamon, cassia, and clove. Curry's popularity in recent decades has spread outward from the Indian subcontinent to figure prominently in international cuisine. Consequently, each culture has adopted curry into its indigenous cooking to suit its own unique tastes and sensibilities. It's a true global phenomenon. It is common to toast curry powder in a dry pan for 30 seconds or until fragrant before using it, to add depth and flavor.

FENNEL SEEDS are native to southern Europe and the Mediterranean area.

They are often confused with anise, which has a similar shape. However, fennel seeds are smaller and green or yellowish brown in color; they are also sweeter and less pungent than anise. The seeds have a distinct licorice flavor and is used widely in Mediterranean cuisine, on the Indian subcontinent, and in the Middle East. They are an essential ingredient of the Oriya spice mixture in Bengali cuisine and in Chinese five-spice powders. In many parts of Pakistan and India roasted fennel seeds are consumed as an after-meal digestive and breath freshener.

GINGER is a rhizome—a plant whose stems grow largely underground in a tangled mass. Native to India and China, it takes its name from the Sanskrit word *stringa-vera*, or "with a body like a horn," meaning an animal horn such as antlers.

Fresh ginger is essential to Asian and Subcontinent cooking. It is used in pickles, chutneys, and curry pastes, and in dried and ground form is a constituent of many curry powders. In the West, dried ginger is mainly used in cakes and cookies, especially ginger snaps and gingerbread, but it's also used in puddings, jams, preserves, and in drinks such as ginger beer, ginger wine, and tea. Ginger root is available in various forms; the most common of which are whole raw roots, powdered (dried ground) ginger, and crystallized ginger.

LEMONGRASS is native to India, but is widely used in Thai and Vietnamese cooking. This is a very pungent herb and is normally used in small amounts. The entire stalk can be used, (though by the time it gets to the supermarket you might want to remove the harder outer layers). The stalk can be sliced very finely and added to soups. It's also used in curries. The light lemon flavor of this grass blends well with garlic, chilies, and cilantro.

MUSTARD SEEDS are native to Asia, and have been used in Indian food for over two thousand years. The French have used mustard seeds as a spice since 800 CE, and it was among the spices collected by the Spanish during their explorations throughout the fifteenth century. Mustard seeds bring a hot and spicy flavor that enhances sauces and salad dressings, and is often used in pickling and boiling vegetables. In Indian cooking, they are fried before use. There are three different types of mustard seeds: yellow, brown, and black. The yellow mustard seeds are the largest and are milder than the others. The brown seeds are most commonly used in Indian cooking, while the black seeds, which were very popular in the West, have now become difficult to find.

NUTMEG is native to the Spice Islands in Indonesia. Nutmeg is a seed encased in an edible fruit that is the size of a peach. It has a sweet, aromatic, nutty flavor that is associated with sweet, spicy dishes such as pies, puddings, custards, cookies, and spice cakes. In fact, in the U.S., that's how it is most often used. But nutmeg combines well with many cheeses, and is included in soufflés and cheese sauces. In soups it works with tomatoes, split peas, and black beans. It complements vegetables like cabbage, spinach, broccoli, beans, onions, and eggplant. Nutmeg loses its flavor and potency very quickly, so if you want to use nutmeg that actually contributes flavor to your recipe, it's best to buy whole nutmeg seeds and grate them by hand as needed.

PAPRIKA is a red powder that is made from grinding dried red bell and/or chili peppers. Hungary, the country where most paprika is produced today, exports six types of paprika, ranging from mild to hot. Paprika powder ranges from bright red to brown and varies from sweet and mild to pungent and hot, depending on the type of pepper used during processing. Sweet paprika is the standard, although it is mild in flavor. The hot paprika gives your taste buds a jolt.

Paprika only releases its flavor when heated, so when you sprinkle it over colorless dishes it improves the food's appearance, but not its flavor. This is why it is often used as a garnish, not a spice. However, you can use it as a flavoring by stirring the powder into some oil before adding it to a recipe. It's important to remember, when using paprika in sauces, that it has a high sugar content and burns easily. Add it only when liquid ingredients are present and do not cook it over high heat for too long.

SAFFRON originates in Western Asia and Persia. It is the world's most expensive spice because it is harvested by hand. It takes about 13,125 threads to get one ounce of the stuff.

It's the star flavor in Spanish paella, and many Indian and Middle Eastern dishes. The threads are usually soaked in hot water before they are added to the dish, which helps them blend in with the other spices. Saffron also imparts a lovely, luminous gold color is used extensively throughout Central Asia to flavor and color festive rice dishes.

SALT is an essential nutrient and mineral needed by the body to maintain electrolyte balance. Its importance as a preservative and nutrient and its ability to enhance the flavor of food gave it a near mystical power.

Civilizations, cities, and entire economies have been built on this oldest geological commodity. Before spice routes were established, merchants traveled "salt routes" and traded and ex-changed it in places where salt was scarce. Sea salt is an excellent all-purpose salt that I use extensively in my kitchen. Kosher salt is a relatively pure salt that contains no iodine or other additives. Its moderately coarse texture makes it an excellent "pinching salt" for cooking. The naturally tinted salt that has appeared on the market in recent years is most often coarse, and must be ground for use.

TURMERIC comes from the root of *Curcuma longa*, a leafy plant in the ginger family. India is the world's primary producer of turmeric, although it is also grown in China and Indonesia. Turmeric is mildly aromatic with a scent reminiscent of orange or ginger, and has a pungent, bitter flavor.

It is often used in place of saffron to provide color, since it is a brilliant orangey yellow. Turmeric has been used medicinally throughout Asia to treat stomach and liver ailments, as well as headaches, due to its anti-inflammatory properties.

Basic Preparation

The trick with tofu is to buy the variety suited to the dish you are preparing. Then you simply press out the water and marinate it. Once you have these steps down, you are sure to make a fabulous tofu dish. Tofu needs to be marinated, but avoid using marinades containing oil, which blocks absorption. Marinated tofu is a snap to prepare on an oiled grill, in a grill pan or under the broiler.

Tofu

Tofu, also known as bean curd, is a protein-rich food that is made from the curds of soybean milk. Off-white in color, it is usually sold in rectangular blocks. Tofu is a staple in the cuisines of many Asian countries.

Tofu comes in a range of consistencies that can suit a variety of different recipes. It is available in either the traditional Chinese block form or the silken Japanese form, which has a custard-like texture. Both forms can be found in soft, firm or extra-firm textures. The soft tofu has a smoother texture and is therefore better suited for salad dressings, sauces and desserts, while firm and extra-firm tofu are best for baking, stir-frying, and grilling.

Only buy organic tofu because soybeans are the most genetically modified (GMO) crops in the United States. The dramatic increase in food allergies, obesity, diabetes, and other food-related diseases is thought to be in direct correlation to the introduction of GMO crops and foods. The best option is to buy from a store that makes fresh tofu every day, and if you live in a big city, there is a good chance you will find this type of store. If you don't live near a store that makes fresh tofu, your next best bet is to find a store that does a brisk business selling pre-packaged tofu. You want the tofu packed in a rectangular, water filled box (or maybe wrapped in plastic), from the refrigerator section. If you open the package and smell more than a tiny whiff of sourness, or the tofu feels slimy, it isn't going to give you a good result in your cooking.

Pressed Tofu

Tofu is packed in water, and it's a lot like a sponge—if you don't press out the old water you can't get any new flavors in. This is really easy; it just takes some advance planning. This procedure assumes the use of water-packed tofu, not the silken kind in the little boxes. Keep in mind: the firmer the tofu, the less water that can be pressed from it.

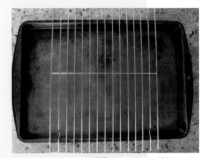

Prep Time: 35 minutes

MATERIALS NEEDED FOR PRESSING
Baking pan
Wire rack
Plate
Paper towels

1 Drain the water from the tofu package.
2 Place the baking pan on flat surface and the wire rack (which will be used to drain the water from the tofu) on it, positioning the rack perpendicular to the pan.
3 Place the tofu on top of the rack, and the plate on top of the tofu. Set some heavy objects (like some cookbooks) on top.
4 Allow the tofu to drain into the pan for 30 minutes.
5 Dry off the tofu with paper towels. This is an important step, which allows the tofu to brown in the skillet. It will also reduce dangerous and unpleasant sputtering when you put it in the skillet.
6 Cut the block into however many slices you want. Marinate and cook the slices according to your recipe.

Legumes

Lentils and beans are nutrient powerhouses that come in a diverse range of flavors and textures. Legumes are a staple for many Middle Eastern, South American, Indian, and Mediterranean dishes. However, almost every country has its own way of using of legumes. They are traditionally combined with grains in almost every corner of the globe.

Low in fat and high in complex carbohydrates, vitamins, and minerals, legumes are an especially important source of protein for vegetarians.

Legumes can be stored for up to a year, but they toughen with time. Be sure to buy from a vendor that does a brisk business to guarantee freshness. Store them in a cool, dry place in an airtight container.

Like many bean lovers, I prefer working with dried beans to the canned version—the flavor is much better. But canned beans can be a respectable substitute if time is short. I've indicated where canned beans can be used in several of the recipes in this book.

Preparing and Cooking Lentils

Lentils, unlike most other legumes, are easy to cook and don't require soaking, so cook as prescribed in the methods to the right. Avoid adding salt to the water when cooking lentils, as this prevents them from softening. Season only when cooked.

Preparing and Cooking Beans

Beans require soaking in room-temperature water, a step that rehydrates them so that they cook evenly. It also reduces the cooking time and enhances the flavor. It was once thought that soaking the beans lessened their gas-producing effects. While this is true to some extent (soaking removes the indigestible complex sugars from the outer coat of the beans), the main reason to soak is to cut down on cooking time.

Basic Method for Cooking Brown and Green Lentils

1 Pour 1 cup (190 g) whole lentils into a strainer and rinse under cold running water. Remove and discard any debris. Transfer to a saucepan.

2 Add 2 cups (500 ml) of water, and bring to a boil over medium-high heat. Reduce the heat and simmer for 40 to 45 minutes, or until tender, adding more water if necessary. Drain and season with salt and freshly-ground pepper.

Basic Method for Cooking Red and Yellow Lentils

1 Pour 1 cup (190 g) whole lentils into a strainer and rinse under cold running water. Remove and discard any debris. Transfer to a saucepan.

2 Add 2½ cups water (625 ml), and bring to a boil over medium-high heat. Reduce the heat slightly and simmer for 20 to 25 minutes, or until the lentils are tender and they have absorbed all the water. Season to taste with salt and freshly-ground pepper.

Basic Methods for Cooking Beans and Chickpeas

1 Pick through the dried beans, discarding any discolored or shriveled ones or any foreign matter. Wash the beans in a strainer under cold running water, and drain.

2 To soak, place the beans in a bowl of fresh cold water. A good rule of thumb is to add three cups (750 ml) of water to each cup of dried beans. The liquid should be about 1 to 2 in (2.5 to 5 cm) above the top of the legumes, and the bowl should be big enough so that the beans can expand a bit. Soak for 12 hours or overnight. [Note: If you are short on time, you can use the quick-soak method instead of the long soaking process. First cook the beans in boiling water for 2 minutes; then remove the pot from the heat. Cover and soak for about 2 hours. Drain and rinse.]

3 Once you have soaked the beans, transfer them to a pot, add enough water to cover the beans by 2 in (5 cm) and bring to a boil. Reduce the heat to a simmer, partially covering the pot, and simmer for one hour, adding more water if too much evaporates and beans become uncovered. If any foam develops, skim it off during the simmering process. If the beans are still hard and no more water remains, add ½ to 1 cup (125 to 250 ml) of hot water and continue to cook until soft. [Note: You must skin the chickpeas after cooking: Drain the hot water and fill the pot with cold water. Let the chickpeas sit until they cool down and the skins of the chickpeas crack open. Rub to loosen the skins and discard them. Pat the chickpeas dry with a paper towel.]

TIPS FOR COOKING BEANS

- Be careful to add salt or acidic ingredients, such as vinegar, tomatoes, or juice, near the end of the cooking time, when the beans are just tender. If these ingredients are added too early, they slow the cooking process.
- Beans are done when they can be easily mashed between two fingers or with a fork.
- To freeze cooked beans for later use, immerse them in cold water until cool, then drain well and freeze.
- One pound of dried beans yields about 5 or 6 cups of cooked beans. A 15-oz (450-g) can of beans makes about 1½ cups (340 g) of cooked beans.
- In some cases, the skin of the bean is too tough to eat. Chickpeas must be skinned after soaking. With fava beans, the skin becomes tough after cooking. You can shell favas using a knife or your fingers; slice into the skin and then it's easy to squeeze out the bean inside.

Grains: Rice and Quinoa

Grains have been cultivated throughout the world for centuries. They are packed with concentrated goodness and are an important source of the complex carbohydrates, protein, vitamins, and minerals that we all need.

For the purpose of this cookbook, I will be focusing on rice and quinoa. Rice was the nutritious and flavorful staple of Silk Road cuisine, while quinoa, a nutrition powerhouse, was a dietary cornerstone in remote parts of South America until its introduction to the rest of the world in the 1980s. Both are gluten free.

Rice

Rice is a grain that belongs to the grass family. It is consumed by nearly half of the world's population and many regions, like Asia, depend on rice as a staple food. In my childhood home, a meal was incomplete if it did not include rice.

Rice is naturally free of fat, cholesterol and sodium. It is a complex carbohydrate containing only 103 calories per half-cup serving. Rice is one of the few foods in the world that is entirely non-allergenic and gluten free.

Rice is considered the most important food crop in India. In fact, according to the ancient Indian practice of Ayurveda, a philosophy of healthy and harmonious living, the basmati variety (one of the most popular in India) actually has some spiritual qualities. Adherents of Ayurveda believe that basmati is *saatvic*, or pure, and therefore beneficial to the body and easy to digest. It is considered an excellent remedy for balancing your *vata* (metabolism) and *pitta* (energy production). By the way, Ayurvedic practice calls for avoiding instant or pre-cooked rice because it has less *prana* (life force) in it. And whether or not you believe in Ayurvedic philosophy, there's no question that processed products do not offer as much nutrition.

Shapes, Sizes, and Colors

Increasingly, people who care about nutrition believe that it's important to choose whole grains. A whole grain of rice has several layers. Only the outermost layer, the hull, is removed to produce what we call brown rice. This process is the least damaging to the nutritional value of the rice and avoids the unnecessary loss of nutrients that occurs with further processing. Brown rice has a lovely, nutty flavor and a chewy texture.

All the recipes in this cookbook call for brown rice because it has the highest nutritional content. For vegetarians, getting the most from your foods is crucial to balanced meals and good health.

In addition to color, rice is classified by the size of its grains: long, medium, and short. Within those three categories, it is further divided by variety.

Long-Grain Rice is the most widely used rice. It's five times as long as it is wide. Most rice grown and consumed in the U.S. is long-grain rice. The grains don't stick together.

Basmati Rice has the longest grain of all, and a translucent appearance. It also

Wild Rice Long Grain Rice Unpolished Rice

Red Rice Parboiled Rice Basmati Rice

Arborio Rice Brown Rice Black Rice

has a distinctive aroma and flavor that Ayurvedic philosophy describes as having a cooling effect, which matches spicy dishes perfectly. Basmati rice has been cultivated at the foot of the Himalayas for centuries. The Hindi name translates to "queen of scents" or "pearl of scents." Brown basmati has more nutrients and has a slightly nuttier flavor than the white variety.

Jasmine Rice is another long-grain aromatic rice. Originally grown in Thailand, it has a soft, slightly sticky texture. It is also called "fragrant rice." It is commonly used in Thai cooking, and

like basmati, nicely offsets the strongly spiced food.

Medium-Grain Rice is two to three times as long as it is wide, and when cooked, it is soft and absorbs the flavors of other food more than long-grain varieties.

Sushi Rice is a medium-grain rice that is flavored with vinegar and used for sushi. When properly cooked, the grains cling together without being mushy. This rice must be polish-washed (by scrubbing the grains against each other gently) to bring out its best flavor.

Short-Grain Rice refers to varieties with grains that are almost round. It is high in amylopectin, a starch that makes the grains soften and cling together when cooked. It is most popular in Asia.

Arborio Rice is a fat, short-grain rice typically used for making Italian risotto. When not rinsed, it releases a starch that gives risotto a buttery texture. This risotto rice can absorb nearly five times its weight in water, which results in its creamy mouthfeel. In this cookbook I use it for a dish similar to risotto, although of Afghan origin, it's called *shola* (page 140).

Glutinous Rice is a short-grain sweet or sticky rice that is a specialty in Thailand. The name is confusing; it might lead one to think it contains gluten, but it doesn't. It's sticky, with a glutinous texture.

Black Rice is also known as black japonica or black sticky rice. Grown mostly in Southeast Asia, this short-grain rice is black due to layers of black bran that surround the kernel. Sometimes under the bran the rice is white, typically, it turns lavender when cooked. Black rice is considered a delicacy in Asia and generally reserved for funerals and celebrations. If you cook this rice with another variety of rice, cook them separately to prevent discoloration.

Wild Rice is a variety you might wonder about. Which category does it fall into? The answer is: none of the above. Wild rice is a coarse grass (and not really a true rice) that is considered a delicacy in many parts of the world. North American Indians were the first to harvest it by paddling to the plants in their canoes. Grown in shallow waters, like marshes, man-made paddies, and stream beds, the wild rice plant grows from three to ten feet tall, holding the traditional rice flower at its peak. American wild rice is medium-to long-grained and has a nutty flavor.

Washing, Soaking, and Cooking Rice

Rice should be washed and soaked before you cook it. Soaking is actually part of the cooking process; it softens the rice and allows the water to penetrate the grains. This prevents sticking and reduces cooking time. It also produces rice with a lovely, light texture, and releases enzymes that make it easier for us to absorb all the nutritional goodness in the rice.

Soaking: Once the rice is washed, it's time to soak. With the rice in the bowl, add enough warm water so that the rice is submerged by about an inch. Use the following soaking times unless directed otherwise in the recipe.

- Long-grain brown rice should be soaked for 2 hours.
- Short-grain brown rice should be soaked for 4 hours.
- Long-grain white rice should be soaked for 30 minutes.
- Short-grain white rice should be soaked for 20 minutes.

Salting: In most cases, the recipes call for soaking in warm water with salt, which is used as a catalyst to decrease cooking time. For every cup of rice, add 1 teaspoon salt and enough warm water so that the rice is submerged by about an inch (2.5 cm).

Rice Yields

- 1 cup uncooked white rice = 3 cups cooked
- 1 cup uncooked brown rice = 3½ cups cooked
- 1 cup wild rice = 3½ to 4 cups cooked
- 1 cup of rice is sufficient for 4 people as a side dish.

Cooking: Do not stir rice while it is cooking because this will cause the grains to break, giving you sticky rice (unless that's the effect you're after, of course). Even sticking the spoon in to taste the rice while it's cooking can have an impact on its structure. The only exceptions to this rule are risotto, and rice cooked in milk for dessert purposes—both need to be stirred.

Cook rice until it reaches the point of being *al dente* (firm but not hard); at this point, the grains are separate and not sticky, and the rice is flavorful. The rice should simmer for 25 minutes without lifting the lid. When done, take the pan off of the heat and allow the rice to sit for five minutes. Fluff the rice with a fork. To test for "doneness," squeeze the rice grains between your fingers. The grains should feel tender and not have a hard center. I've called for brown rice in this book. If you prefer long-grain white rice, you can reduce the cooking time by 15 minutes.

Basic Silk Road Rice Variations

Along the Silk Road, each community developed its own way of preparing rice. Some colored their rice with spices, while others added dried fruits for sweetness. Still others garnished with nuts for crunchiness. As an alternative to expensive meat, beans were often added. Rice was also used as a filling for *dolmas* (stuffed vegetables) and made into puddings. (The earliest gluten-free desserts!)

There are four primary methods of cooking rice along the Silk Road based on the Persian method. Several appear in this book in the chapter titled "Rice Dishes" (page 128).

Steamed Rice—*Chelow* (Farsi) is rice that is carefully prepared by first soaking and parboiling, at which point the water is drained and the rice is steamed with a towel. This method results in fluffy rice with the grains separated and not sticky. A golden rice crust called *tahdig* develops at the bottom of the pot. The name literally means "bottom of the pot" in Farsi.

Polo (Farsi) is rice that is cooked in exactly the same manner as *chelow*, except that after the rice is drained, other ingredients are layered with it and they are then steamed together. *Polo* has its origin in Persia, but spread eastward, morphing into the Indian *pilau*, and westward, where it became Spanish paella and Italian risotto. You will find many *polo* recipes (with their varying spellings) in this cookbook.

Boiled Rice—*Kateh* (Farsi) is rice that is boiled until the water is absorbed. This is the traditional dish of Northern Iran.

Boiled Rice with a Towel—*Damy* (Farsi) is rice that is cooked in almost the same fashion as *kateh*, except that the heat is reduced just before boiling and a towel is placed between the lid and the pot to prevent steam from escaping. (*Damy* literally means "simmered" in Farsi.)

Quinoa

Technically quinoa is not a true grain, but the seed of the goosefoot plant. It is used as a grain and substituted for grains because of its cooking characteristics. The name comes from the Spanish spelling of the *Quenchua* name *kinwa* or occasionally *qin-wah*.

Quinoa has a delightful characteristic that is all its own; as it cooks, the outer germ around each grain twists outward, forming a little white spiral tail, which is attached to the kernel. The grain itself is soft and delicate and the tail is crunchy. It has a fluffy consistency and a mild, delicate, slightly nutty flavor.

Before you cook quinoa, the seeds must be rinsed to remove their bitter resin-like coating, which is called *saponin*. Quinoa is rinsed before it is packaged and sold, but it is best to rinse again at home before use to remove any of the powdery residue that may remain on the seeds. This residue looks like soapy "suds" when the seeds are swished in water. Placing quinoa in a strainer and rinsing thoroughly with running water easily washes the saponin from the seeds.

The quinoa seed is high in protein, calcium, and iron, and it's a relatively good source of vitamin E and several of the B vitamins. It contains an almost perfect balance of all eight essential amino acids needed for tissue development in humans. It is exceptionally high in lysine, cystine, and methionine, all of which are amino acids not found in high concentrations in other grains. It is a good complement for legumes, which are likewise often low in methionine and cystine. The protein in quinoa is considered to be a complete protein due to the presence of all eight essential amino acids, making it one of the very few plant foods to offer complete protein. (Some types of wheat come close to matching quinoa's protein content, but grains such as barley, corn, and rice generally have less than half of the protein of quinoa.)

Because of its relatively high oil and fat content, quinoa grains and flour should be stored in glass jars in the refrigerator. Use the grains within a year and flour within three months.

Perfect Quinoa

Here is a procedure that will ensure that your quinoa turns out perfectly every time. This recipe calls for one cup of quinoa, but you can use any amount—just use one part quinoa to one and a half parts liquid. Use the liquid that best suits your dish.

Makes 4 side dish servings

INGREDIENTS
1 cup (170 g) quinoa
1½ cups (375 ml) Vegetable Broth (page 45), water, or other liquid

1 If you are working with unrinsed quinoa, start off by soaking it. You can soak it for an hour or more without a negative impact, but 15 minutes will do the trick. After soaking, transfer the quinoa to a strainer and rinse.
2 Pour the quinoa into a saucepan and add the liquid, bring to a simmer and then reduce the heat to low. Cover and cook for 30 to 35 minutes. Remove from the heat and let stand, covered, for 5 more minutes. Fluff and serve.

Food Preservation: Freezing

Try freezing summer surplus to extend the rewards of the season! Don't wait for a huge collection—freeze in small batches to save it for later.

Why preserve when you can just run to the store? Preserving locally grown produce is a way to live locally and control the cost and quality of your food—and freezing is the simplest way to extend the life of food.

Selecting the Freshest Produce

Start with produce that is absolutely top quality and at the peak of freshness. If you freeze vegetables when they are immature, they will be soft and shriveled when you cook them. If they are over-ripe when you freeze them, they will be stringy and tough when cooked.

Selecting Freezer Containers

Containers should be moisture-vapor resistant, durable, easy to seal, and should not become brittle at low temperatures.

Wraps: For flexible packaging, use heavy-duty aluminum foil.

Freezer Bags: Use freezer bags for items that will not clump when frozen, such as peas. Once you fill the bag, remove as much air as possible to prevent oxidation. Shape sealed bags and stack them in the freezer like bricks.

Containers: Use glass or plastic, rectangular or square nesting containers. You can also use canning jars—with straight sides only; to avoid cracking when freezing, and facilitate removing the contents.

Packaging, Labeling and Storing

Leave space between the food and lid to allow for expansion. Before closing the container, make sure the sealing edges are clean. Label the container with the name of the food and the date.

Freezing Fruit

Unsweetened fruits deteriorate faster than those packed in sugar or syrup. Freeze packaged fruits as quickly as possible at 0°F or below to maintain quality for 8–12 months; citrus fruits and juices, for 4–6 months. To speed the process, place items against the cold freezer surfaces.

Freeze only the freshest fruit. Sort, gently rinse, and drain fruits, discarding any that are green or of poor quality. Do not allow fruit to soak in the water. Prepare fruits as they will be used: stemmed, pitted, peeled, or sliced. Prepare enough fruit for only a few containers at a time, especially those fruits that darken rapidly. Be wary of using iron utensils or chipped enamelware, as metallic off-flavors can result.

While not necessary, you can often achieve superior texture and flavor by preserving fruit in sugar or syrup. Those packed in syrup work well in uncooked desserts; those packed in dry sugar or unsweetened contain less liquid and are good for cooking.

Types of Packaging

There are various ways to pack fruit for freezing.

Honey Syrup—Best for keeping fruit firm for serving uncooked as dessert. Use a mild-flavored honey, like clover, locust, or alfalfa. For a thin syrup, dissolve 1 cup of honey in 3 cups of boiling water. Chill the syrup before adding it to the fruit. Shake a filled container to settle the contents. Pour the syrup over the fruit, completely covering it. If the fruit is well packed in a container, ½ cup of syrup will be enough for a pint container and 1 cup will top off a quart container. Cover with waxed paper to compact the contents and seal with the lid. Cover and refrigerate leftover syrup for up to a month.

Honey Pack—Straight honey improves the flavor, texture and color of your fruit. As the fruit freezes, its juices mix with the honey to create syrup, and the fruit absorbs the syrup and stays firm. Honey packs work best with fruits that are naturally juicy, like peaches. Cut the fruit into slices, place in a bowl and gently mix with the honey until the juices are drawn out. Then pack for freezing.

Sugar Pack—Sprinkle sugar over the fruit and mix gently until the juice is drawn out and the sugar has dissolved. Soft sliced fruits such as peaches, strawberries, figs, seeded grapes, plums, and cherries will yield sufficient syrup for covering if the fruit is layered with sugar and allowed to stand for 15 minutes. Some small whole fruits may be coated with sugar and frozen.

Dry Pack—Small whole fruits, such as berries, freeze well without sugar.

Tray Pack—This is an alternative that can make the fruit easier to remove from the container. Simply spread a single layer of prepared fruit on a shallow tray and freeze. Once frozen, promptly package it in a freezer container or freezer bag, seal, and return it to the freezer. The pieces should remain loose, so they can be poured from the container and the package resealed.

Other Unsweetened Packs—Fruit can also be packaged in water or apple juice, but the fruits freeze harder and take longer to thaw, and quality can suffer. However, some fruits such as raspberries, blueberries, steamed apple, gooseberries, currants, cranberries, rhubarb, and figs maintain integrity without sugar.

Preventing Discoloration

Some fruits—such as peaches, apples, pears, and apricots—will darken quickly when exposed to air and during freezing. They may also lose flavor when thawed. To prevent this, you can dip the fruit in acidulated water—that is, water to which some sort of acid has been added. Try ascorbic acid (vitamin C), available at most drug or grocery stores, by adding 3 grams (six 500 mg vitamin C tablets) per gallon of water. Lemon juice is handy and also works well. Mix ¼ cup lemon juice into 1 gallon of water. For either solution, soak fruit for two minutes, and then proceed to freeze as desired. If you are using a dry pack, let the fruit dry a bit before freezing.

A Guide to Preparing Fruit for Freezing

APPLES Wash, core and peel. Cut in halves, quarters or slices. Acidulate. Use a dry pack, sugar pack, honey pack, or honey syrup.

APRICOTS Freeze them whole, halved or quartered, and with or without pits. (The pit adds flavor.) To freeze whole without the skin, dip in boiling water for 15 to 20 seconds; then plunge into ice water. The skin should slide off easily. Acidulate. Use a honey pack.

AVOCADOS Best frozen as a purée; peel, remove the pit, and mash the pulp with 1 tablespoon lemon juice. Use a dry pack.

BANANAS AND PLAN-TAINS Freeze bananas that have turned brown and use them for baking. Freeze in the skin or peeled. Use a dry pack.

BERRIES Wash in cold water and lift out of the washing water. Remove any that are wrinkled, damaged, or discolored. Use a tray pack and then transfer to a container. Or freeze in a honey pack, honey syrup, sugar pack, or unsweetened pack.

CHERRIES Wash in cold water. Remove any that are wrinkled, damaged, or discolored. Pit them. Use a tray pack and transfer to freezer bags.

CITRUS FRUITS Peel and remove as much membrane and white pith surrounding the sections as possible. Use a dry pack, placing a double layer of waxed paper between layers for easy removal. Or use a honey pack, honey syrup, or sugar pack.

COCONUT Pierce with an ice pick to drain out the liquid; reserve it. Then use a hammer and tap all around the middle until it splits. Cut out meat and shred it or cut it into large pieces. Pack in its own liquid.

FIGS Wash and remove the stems. If the skin is thin, peel it off; otherwise leave it on. Keep whole or cut in half and scoop out the seeds. Use honey pack, honey syrup, sugar pack, or unsweetened pack. If puréeing the figs, use honey syrup.

GRAPES Wash in cold water and remove the stems. Remove any that are wrinkled, damaged, or discolored. Use a tray pack and transfer to a freezer container.

KIWI Peel and cut into slices. Use a honey pack or sugar pack.

MANGOES Wash in cold water, peel and cut out the pit. Cut in ¼-inch (6 mm) slices. Acidulate. Use a honey pack, honey syrup, or sugar pack.

MELONS These will freeze well, except for watermelon. Peel and remove seeds and cut into slices, cubes, or balls. Use a tray pack, honey pack, honey syrup, or sugar pack.

NECTARINES Wash in cold water and peel. Halve the fruit and remove the pits. Acidulate and drain. Use a honey pack, honey syrup, or sugar pack.

PEARS These don't freeze well. If you do freeze, wash, core, peel, and halve first. Acidulate and drain. Use a honey pack, honey syrup, or sugar pack.

PINEAPPLE Peel and cut into any shape you desire. Pack in its own juice in a freezer container.

PLUMS AND PRUNES These do not freeze well; however, if you do freeze them, wash in cold water and remove the pits. Leave whole or cut up. Use a dry pack, honey pack or sugar pack.

RHUBARB Prepare stalks that are red and crisp. Remove the leaves and cut off woody ends. Cut into ½ to 1-inch (2.5 to 5-cm) chunks. Use a tray pack, and transfer to freezer bags.

STRAWBERRIES Wash in cold water and remove the hulls. Remove any that are wrinkled, damaged, or discolored and let the berries dry. Cut into any size or keep whole. Use a tray pack and transfer to freezer bags.

Freezing Vegetables

Freeze vegetables that are at their peak of flavor and texture. Wash your vegetables thoroughly in cold water. Sort by size for blanching and packing.

Blanching—You must parboil most vegetables prior to freezing. Blanching neutralizes spoiling enzymes, softens, sanitizes, brightens, and retains vitamins. Timing varies with the vegetable and its size. Refer to the chart to the right for blanching times.

Water Blanching—Boiling water removes bacteria, yeast, mold, and chemical residues. Use a blancher with basket and cover, or fit a wire basket into a large kettle with a lid. Use a gallon of water per pound of prepared vegetables. Put the vegetables in a blanching basket and lower into vigorously boiling water. Cover and keep the heat high for the duration of blanching time. Start timing once the water returns to a boil.

Steam Blanching—Use for broccoli, pumpkin, sweet potatoes, and summer and winter squash. Use a steamer pot with a tight lid and a basket that holds the food at least three inches above the bottom of the kettle. Pour an inch or two of water in the kettle and bring to a boil. Put the vegetables into the steamer basket in a single layer so that the heat permeates quickly. Cover the pot and keep the heat high. Start timing as soon as the lid is on.

Cooking and Baking—Some vegetables, like beets, need to be cooked before freezing. Others, like spaghetti squash (and puréed pumpkin), must be baked.

The Ice-Water Plunge—Vegetables must be cooled quickly to stop the cooking process. Prepare a large container of chilled water while the vegetables are blanching. Plunge the vegetables into the chilled water and leave them there for the same amount of time that you blanched them. Drain vegetables after cooling.

Packing for Freezing—For vegetables, use meal-size plastic freezer containers and freezer bags. Pack items tightly to reduce the air in the package, but leave a ½-inch gap at the top to allow for expansion. This provision for headroom is not necessary for foods such as broccoli, asparagus and Brussels sprouts, which do not pack tightly in containers.

A Guide to Preparing Vegetables for Freezing

ARTICHOKES Wash and remove the outer leaves. Cut off the bottom end of the stem and trim the top. *Water-blanch for 8 to 10 minutes; follow with ice-water plunge.* Let dry and then dry-pack in freezer bags.

ASPARAGUS Wash the spears and trim the ends. Use a vegetable peeler to remove tough parts. *Water-blanch for 2 to 4 minutes; follow with ice-water plunge.* Pat dry and pack in freezer containers.

BEETS Scrub the beets and trim the tops. Beets must be cooked before freezing. Preheat oven to 400°F and place the beets in an ovenproof dish and cover with foil. *Bake for 1 hour or until beets are tender.* Cool the baked beets, skin them and pack in freezer containers.

BROCCOLI Trim away all leaves and wash away any insects or debris. Cut the stalks to a uniform size. *Water-blanch for 3 to 4 minutes or steam-blanch for 6 minutes; follow with ice-water plunge.* Let dry and pack in freezer containers.

BRUSSELS SPROUTS Wash and trim the outer leaves. *Water-blanch for 3 to 5 minutes; follow with ice-water plunge.* Pat dry and pack in freezer bags.

CABBAGE Wash the head and discard outer leaves. To remove whole leaves for freezing, cut around the core of the cabbage to loosen them. You can also cut it into wedges. *Water-blanch* until the outer layer is translucent. Cool for 5 minutes and blanch again. If you are using cabbage wedges, blanch and cool 2 minutes; follow with ice-water plunge. Let dry and pack leaves flat with wax paper separating the layers. Or transfer wedges to freezer containers.

CARROTS Wash and peel if desired. *Water-blanch for 5 minutes ; follow with ice-water plunge.* Let dry and pack in freezer containers.

CAULIFLOWER Discard the leaves and stems and wash the head carefully. Break into florets. *Water-blanch for 4 to 6 minutes; follow with ice-water plunge.* Let dry and pack in freezer bags.

CELERY Wash, peel and cut into cubes or rounds. *Water-blanch for 4 minutes; follow with ice-water plunge.* Let dry and pack in freezer bags.

CORN Remove husks and silk from ears. Leave cobs whole, or just retain kernels. *Water-blanch for 5 to 8 minutes; follow with ice-water plunge.* Pat dry and pack in freezer bags.

EGGPLANT Wash, peel and cut into ½-inch (1.25-cm) thick slices or cubes. Squeeze lemon juice over them to prevent discoloration. *Water-blanch for 3 minutes; follow with ice-water plunge.* Let dry and freeze on a tray with wax paper for easy removal. Pack in freezer containers or bags.

GREEN BEANS Trim off the ends with a knife and remove any that are wrinkled, dam-

aged or discolored. *Water-blanch for 4 minutes; follow with ice-water plunge.* Pat dry and freeze on a tray; then pack in freezer bags.

LEEKS Trim, wash thoroughly, and cut into chunks. *Water-blanch for 1 minute; follow with ice-water plunge.* Let dry and pack in freezer bags.

LIMA BEANS Discard any beans that are not perfect. *Water-blanch for 2 to 4 minutes; follow with ice-water plunge.* Pat dry and freeze on a tray; then pack in freezer bags.

OKRA Remove the stems. *Water-blanch for 1 to 3 minutes; follow with ice-water plunge.* Pat dry and pack in freezer bags.

PARSNIPS Wash, peel, and slice. Blanch, let dry and transfer to freezer containers. *Water-blanch for 1 to 2 minutes; follow with ice-water plunge.* Pat dry and pack in freezer bags.

PEAS Remove the peas from the pods. *Water-blanch 1 to 2 minutes; follow with ice-water plunge.* Pat dry and freeze on a tray; then pack in freezer bags.

PEPPERS Wash and remove the stems, pith and seeds. Cut as desired or leave whole. *No need to blanch.* Pack in freezer bags.

SOYBEANS These beans are blanched in their pods and shelled afterward. *Water-blanch the pods for 5 minutes; follow with ice-water plunge.* Pat the pods dry; then shell the beans and pack in freezer bags.

SPAGHETTI SQUASH Wash, slit in half lengthwise and scoop out the seeds. Preheat the oven to 375°F and place squash cut-side up in a shallow baking pan. *Bake for 30 minutes.* Cool and pull a fork through the flesh to remove the strands. Store the strands in freezer bags.

SUMMER SQUASH Wash, halve, remove the seeds, and cut into cubes. *Steam-blanch for 2 to 3 minutes; follow with ice-water plunge.* Let dry and pack in freezer containers.

TOMATOES Freeze tomatoes only to use in soups, stews or sauces. Wash and stem them. Pack washed tomatoes immediately in freezer bags.

TURNIPS AND RUTABAGAS Cut off the tops and reserve for another use if desired. Wash the roots and peel. Cut into cubes. *Water-blanch for 1 to 2 minutes; follow with ice-water plunge.* Pat dry and pack in freezer bags.

WINTER SQUASH AND PUMPKIN Wash, halve and remove the seeds. For purée, preheat the oven to 350°F, place in a baking dish, and bake until soft. To freeze cubes, peel and cut into cubes. *For purée, bake for 30 to 40 minutes or until soft. For cubes, steam-blanch for 15 minutes; follow with ice-water plunge.* For purée, cool and scrape the flesh out of the baked shell; pack in freezer containers. For cubes, let dry and pack in freezer containers.

Chapter 1
Bases, Condiments & Other Useful Recipes

This chapter presents flavorful and easy-to-prepare sauces and condiments that you would normally find in your local supermarket, as well as useful techniques to get the most out of your ingredients. Learning to prepare these simple recipes is more economical and healthier than purchasing them, especially considering all of the flavor enhancers and preservatives that are added to many packaged foods. Most of the recipes here can be kept for later use by sealing and storing them in the fridge. The recipes in this chapter will be quick-cooking allies for you to use and enjoy often.

Hummus Dip V GF

The Mediterranean dip made from chickpeas, lemon juice, and garlic has become ubiquitous in the West. The name comes from the Arabic word for chickpeas. It made its debut more than a millennium ago, and has gained fans ever since; it is now available in most major supermarkets. Hummus is traditionally scooped with flatbread (such as pita) and served as part of a *meze* (appetizer spread) or as an accompaniment to falafel and vegetables. Garnishes include chopped tomato, cucumber, coriander leaves, parsley, caramelized onions, sautéed mushrooms, olive oil, paprika, olives, pickles, and pine nuts. Serve the spread on a plate dressed with your favorite topping and call it your own.

Prep time: 5 minutes, plus 12 hours for soaking the beans
Cook time: 45 minutes
Makes 2 cups

INGREDIENTS

¾ cup (150 g) dried chickpeas, or one 15-oz (425-g) can chickpeas, rinsed and drained

¼ cup (65 ml) extra-virgin olive oil, or more as needed

Freshly squeezed juice of 2 lemons

¼ cup (65 ml) water, plus more if needed

5 cloves garlic, peeled

1 teaspoon salt

1 Soak, skin, and cook the chickpeas according to the instructions on page 29.
2 Pour the cooked chickpeas, oil, lemon juice, water, garlic, and salt into a food processor fitted with a metal blade, and process until creamy. If the consistency is too thick, add a little more water.

Sesame Seed Paste V GF

TAHINI

This is the main ingredient in Tahini Sauce (page 47), as well as Minted Beet Salad (page 87) and Red Cabbage Slaw with Tahini Dressing (page 95), to name a few. If kept in a tightly sealed jar in the refrigerator it can last up to 3 months.

Prep Time: 5 minutes
Makes ⅓ cup

INGREDIENTS

4 tablespoons sesame seeds
1 teaspoon sesame oil
¼ teaspoon salt
4 tablespoons warm water

1 Pour the sesame seeds into a blender or food processor and grind until smooth.
2 Add the oil and salt. Process until combined.
3 With the blades engaged, add the water in a very slow, steady stream and blend until smooth. Check to make sure that you are adding just the right amount of water so that the mixture is not runny but has a pasty consistency. Store in an airtight container in a cool, dry place for up to 3 months.

Tomato Paste V GF

This recipe has few ingredients and is very easy to make, but it takes quite a bit of time. I make this paste when my CSA delivers over 5 pounds (2¼ kg) of tomatoes, and I have to extend their use. Use overripe tomatoes (just before they really have to be thrown out) to get the best results. Note that you will need several sterilized jars.

Prep Time: 10 minutes, plus 12 hours to strain
Cook Time: 35 minutes
Makes 2 to 3 cups

INGREDIENTS

4 lbs (2 kg) end-of-season, overripe tomatoes, peeled
1 sweet red pepper (pimiento or red bell), seeded and pith removed
1 tablespoon salt
Extra-virgin olive oil, for storing

1 Process the tomatoes and pepper in a food processor fitted with a metal blade until pulpy.
2 Transfer to a pot, set it over medium-high heat, and bring to a boil. Boil for 2 to 3 minutes.
3 Line a sieve with a piece of tulle or a coffee filter and set it over a bowl. Pour in the mixture and let it drain for 12 hours in the refrigerator to remove all excess liquid.
4 Preheat the oven to 300°F (150°C). Transfer the mixture to a glass or ceramic baking dish and stir in the salt. Let it sit until it reaches room temperature. Then bake for 30 minutes, or until the tomatoes have turned into a thick paste.
5 Spoon into sterilized glass jars, taking care to avoid creating air pockets, and top with ¼-in (6-mm) of the oil (enough to cover completely). Store in the refrigerator until ready to use and refrigerate any leftovers. These will keep well until next year's tomato crop is ready! As the tomato paste is used, add more oil to the top as needed.

North African Chili Paste V GF

HARISSA

Deriving from the Arabic word for "to break," as in breaking down a medley of hot chili peppers to form a paste, *harissa* is a scorching hot sauce that is used sparingly in dishes for a little (or large) jolt.

Prep Time: 20 minutes
Makes 1⅓ cups

INGREDIENTS

18 assorted dried hot red chili peppers (such as ancho, arbol, cayenne, or guajillo) stemmed, slit lengthwise, pith removed and seeded

12 cloves garlic, peeled

1 tablespoon ground cumin

1 tablespoon salt

½ cup (115 ml) extra-virgin olive oil

1 Soak the chilies in a bowl of hot water for about 30 minutes, or until softened. Drain.
2 Pulse the chilies, garlic, cumin, and salt in a food processor. Drizzle the oil in slowly until the mixture forms a thick paste.
3 Transfer to a jar and cover. Store in the refrigerator for up to 4 months.

Raita GF

This is a yogurt and cucumber condiment that originated in Pakistan and India; it's a must-add ingredient in spicy Indian dishes. Similar to Greek *tzatziki*, this soothes the palate with cooling cucumber and mint, and adds a refreshing balance to any curry dish.

Prep Time: 20 minutes
Cook Time: 5 minutes
Makes 3 cups

INGREDIENTS

2 cucumbers, peeled and finely chopped

½ teaspoon cumin seeds

2 cups (500 g) plain whole-milk yogurt

2 tablespoons green onions (scallions), trimmed and finely sliced

1 tablespoon freshly squeezed lemon juice

Salt, to taste

Freshly ground black pepper, to taste

1 tablespoon chopped fresh mint, for garnish

1 Place the chopped cucumber in a colander, sprinkle with salt and let it stand for 15 minutes. Rinse with cold water and drain. Pat the cucumbers dry with paper towels.
2 In the meantime, dry-roast the cumin seeds for about a minute, until they pop, in a small skillet set over medium-high heat. Watch carefully so they don't burn. Remove from the heat and set aside.
3 Combine the cucumber, yogurt, green onions, lemon juice, salt, and pepper in a medium-size bowl.
4 To bruise the cumin seeds, place them on a work surface, place the blade of a large chef's knife on top of them and press down on it with the heel of your hand to crush them lightly. Sprinkle the crushed seeds over the cucumber-yogurt mixture.
5 Serve chilled, garnish with the mint.

Oven Roasted Nuts

It's the little things that transform the merely good to great, and in the kitchen, roasting nuts catapults an ordinary dish to extraordinary. The difference between a complex golden roasted nut and a sorry-looking blanched specimen is no small thing.

Prep Time: 5 minutes
Cook Time: 5 minutes

1 Preheat oven to 350°F (175°C). Arrange the nuts in a single layer on a baking sheet.
2 Roast for about 5 minutes. Remove from oven and stir gently to prevent burning. Return to the oven and roast for another 5 minutes. The nuts are ready when they are golden and fragrant.

Toasted Seeds and Spices

Gently toasting seeds and spices greatly enhances their flavors by heating the natural oils within.

STOVETOP METHOD
Prep Time: 1 minute
Cook Time: 1 minute

Set a small dry saucepan over medium heat, toast the seeds until they start to pop; this will take less than a minute, so watch them carefully and remove from the heat before they burn.

OVEN METHOD
Prep Time: 1 minute
Cook Time: 1 minute

1 Preheat the oven to 350°F (175°C).
2 Place the seeds on a sheet of aluminum foil in a single layer and bake for 10 minutes, turning after the first 5 minutes. Keep an eye on them to make sure they don't burn.

Za'atar Spice Mix

This spice blend is a generic name for a Middle Eastern mixture of herbs. *Za'atar* is popular in Arab cuisine and throughout the Middle East. It can even be used in lieu of salt for flavoring salads and yogurt dips.

Prep Time: 5 minutes
Makes ½ cup

INGREDIENTS

1 tablespoon toasted sesame seeds (see Toasted Seeds and Spices, below left)

4 tablespoons dried sumac

2 tablespoons dried thyme

2 tablespoons dried marjoram

2 tablespoons dried oregano

1 teaspoon coarse salt

1 Grind the sesame seeds in a food processor or with mortar and pestle. Add the sumac, thyme, marjoram, oregano, and salt, and mix well.
2 Store the za'atar in a cool, dark place in a sealable plastic bag or in an airtight container. When stored properly, za'atar will keep for 3 to 6 months.

Vegetable Broth v GF

A vegetable stock is vital as the foundation of many soups. Simmering a pot of stock, engulfed in an array of comforting aromas, is just one of the ways I enjoy a leisurely day. The process of making vegetable broth is fairly easy and the results are cheaper and tastier than store-bought versions. All you have to do is brown some vegetables, add herbs and spices, cover with water and simmer. It's really that simple. The ingredient list is also pretty flexible. Taste will not be compromised if you only have one carrot rather than two. You can add vegetables of your choice to the ingredient list below. A general rule of thumb is this: for every 4 cups (1 liter) of stock, to use 2 tablespoons of fresh herbs. Use salt sparingly, since the stock reduces as it simmers and the flavors intensify. Store in the fridge for up to a week or in the freezer for up to 3 months.

Prep Time: 15 minutes
Cook Time: 45 minutes
Makes 9 cups

INGREDIENTS

2 tablespoons oil

1 large onion, quartered

2 carrots, cut into large chunks

2 potatoes, cut into large chunks

2 celery stalks (including leaves), cut into large chunks

8 cloves garlic

½ cup (15 g) chopped fresh parsley (including stems)

2 bay leaves

½ teaspoon salt

¼ teaspoon freshly ground black pepper

2 quarts (2 liters) water

1 Heat the oil and sauté the onions, carrots, potatoes, celery and garlic in a large stockpot. Stir for 5 to 10 minutes, or until the vegetables have softened a bit and the onions are translucent.

2 Add the parsley, bay leaves, salt, pepper, and water and bring to a boil. Reduce the heat and simmer, uncovered, for 30 minutes, or until the vegetables are soft and the liquid has thickened significantly. Do not stir during the simmering process, as this will cause the vegetables to break down and cloud the soup stock.

3 Let it cool and then strain. Discard the vegetables and store the broth in the refrigerator. If you are freezing this broth, allow the stock to cool completely and pour it into ice cube trays. Pop out the cubes when they are completely frozen and store in freezer bags.

Shawarma Spice Mix

This is the classic Middle Eastern spice blend that creates that smoky charred taste that often you will find rubbed on *shawarma*, thin slices of meat cooked on a rotating skewer.

Prep Time: 5 minutes
Cook Time: 3 minutes
Makes ⅓ cup

INGREDIENTS

1 tablespoon ground cumin
1 tablespoon ground coriander
1 tablespoon garlic powder
½ tablespoon paprika
1 teaspoon ground turmeric
1 teaspoon freshly ground black pepper
½ teaspoon ground cloves
½ teaspoon ground cayenne pepper
½ teaspoon ground cinnamon

1 Preheat the oven to 300°F (150°C).
2 Spread out all of the ingredients on a baking sheet and roast for 3 minutes. Remove from the oven and let the mixture cool completely. Store in an airtight container for up to a month.

Applesauce

There is nothing better than homemade applesauce prepared with hand-picked apples, and it is so easy to do! Be sure to use sweet cooking apples, such as Golden Delicious, Jonagold, Granny Smith, Fuji, Jonathan, Mcintosh, or Gravenstein; you can mix and match as you please. For a smooth applesauce, run the cooked apples through a food processor. Serve either hot or chilled. This recipe will keep in the refrigerator for 7 to 10 days. It lasts up to one year in the freezer.

Prep Time: 15 minutes
Cook Time: 45 minutes
Makes 3 cups

INGREDIENTS

6 sweet apples, peeled, cored, and quartered
Freshly squeezed juice of 1 lemon
One 4-in (10-cm) cinnamon stick
4 tablespoons of packed brown sugar
1 cup (250 ml) of water

1 Put the apples, lemon juice, cinnamon stick, brown sugar, and water into a large pot set over high heat, cover and bring to a boil. Reduce the heat and simmer for 20 to 30 minutes.
2 Remove from the heat and remove the cinnamon stick. Mash the apples with a potato masher for a rustic feel or run through a food processor for a smoother consistency.

Tahini Sauce V GF

The name comes from the root of the Arabic for "to grind," as in grinding to make a thick paste from sesame seeds. It originated as a by-product of sesame oil production, but became a delicacy in its own right. When stored, tahini sauce will separate. Just stir before using to bring it back to the proper emulsion. It will keep in the fridge from 7 to 10 days in a sealed container.

Prep Time: 5 minutes
Makes 1 cup

INGREDIENTS

1 cup Sesame Seed Paste (tahini—page 42)
½ cup (125 ml) freshly squeezed lemon juice
½ cup (125 ml) water, plus more if needed
2 cloves garlic, crushed
¾ teaspoon salt

Combine the tahini, lemon juice, water, garlic, and salt in a medium bowl. Stir until smooth. You can add more water, 4 tablespoons at a time, if the consistency is too thick.

Duck Sauce V GF

Duck sauce is a sweet and sour citrus-flavored sauce consisting of a combination of plums, peaches, and apricots combined with sugar, vinegar, ginger, and chilies. It has a somewhat gelatinous texture and a gently spicy undertone. It's commonly used as a dipping sauce for appetizers and as a base for marinades.

Prep Time: 15 minutes
Cook Time: 1 hour
Makes 2 to 3 cups

INGREDIENTS

5 cups (1 kg) coarsely chopped pitted apricots, peaches, and plums
1 cup (250 ml) water
¾ cup (185 ml) apple juice
1 teaspoon gluten-free soy sauce
1 tablespoon apricot preserves
½ cup (100 g) packed light brown sugar
½ teaspoon garlic powder
½ teaspoon red pepper flakes

1 Combine the fruit, water, apple juice, soy sauce, apricot preserves, brown sugar, garlic powder, and red pepper flakes in a large pot set over medium heat. Reduce the heat and simmer for 40 minutes. Remove from the heat and allow it to cool.

2 Once it has cooled sufficiently, blend the mixture with an immersion blender until it is completely smooth. Cover and refrigerate in a sealed container for up to 5 days.

Mango Chutney

V GF

This is a gentle combination of sweet and sour with a peppery spiciness. It's great with stews, burgers, and cold dishes. Keep in the refrigerator for up to two weeks.

Prep Time: 10 minutes
Cook Time: 35 minutes
Makes 2 cups

INGREDIENTS

1 tablespoon oil

1 small onion, diced

2 cloves garlic, minced

One 1-in (2.5-cm) piece fresh ginger, peeled and finely grated (about 1 tablespoon)

1 cup (250 ml) white vinegar

¾ cup (90 g) brown sugar

½ teaspoon red pepper flakes

3 very ripe mangoes, peeled, pitted, and roughly chopped

4 tablespoons raisins

Tofu Mayonnaise

V GF

This soy-based version of the classic mayo filled with saturated fat is a much healthier version that is filled with monounsaturated fats. Use it in sandwiches, as a crudités spread, or as a salad dressing base. Can be stored in the refrigerator for up to a week. If the mayonnaise separates just whisk to combine again.

Prep Time: 5 minutes
Makes 1½ cups

INGREDIENTS

One 12-oz (350-g) package of silken tofu

3 tablespoons freshly squeezed lemon juice

2 tablespoons extra-virgin olive oil

1 teaspoon mustard

½ teaspoon salt

Combine the tofu, lemon juice, oil, mustard, and salt in a food processor and emulsify until blended.

1 Heat the olive oil in a saucepan set over medium heat. Sauté the onion, garlic, and ginger, stirring occasionally, until softened.

2 Stir in the vinegar, brown sugar, and red pepper flakes. Cook for 2 to 3 minutes, until the spices are fragrant.

3 Add the chopped mango and raisins, reduce the heat and cook for 15 to 20 minutes, or until softened with consistency of a jam. Remove from the heat and allow it to cool before storing in a sealed jar.

Coconut Milk

V GF

This sweet "milk," made from a mature coconut, is 1 part grated coconut and 1 part water. I use coconut milk extensively in this cookbook as a base for curries, in lieu of cream, and as a dairy substitute in desserts. It is so easy to make and store.

Prep Time: 5 minutes
Cook Time: 15 minutes
Makes 2 cups

INGREDIENTS

2 cups (500 ml) water

2 cups (150 g) grated fresh or frozen coconut

1 Bring the water to a boil in a large saucepan. Stir in the coconut and then remove from the heat. Cover and let it cool.
2 Purée with an immersion blender. Line a sieve with cheesecloth and set it over a bowl. Pour the purée into the sieve and squeeze the cloth to extract the liquid. Remove the cheesecloth and use the coconut milk right away or store it in the refrigerator, covered, for up to 2 days. Shake before using.

How to Remove Coconut Meat

1 Hold the coconut in the palm of your hand over a sink or large bowl. The bowl will catch the coconut juice when the coconut splits open.
2 Follow the seam to the equator of the coconut. Using the blunt edge (not the blade) of a heavy knife (for example, a chef's knife, meat cleaver, machete) tap firmly around its equator as you rotate the coconut in the palm of your hand.
3 Continue to tap and rotate until the coconut splits completely open. If it's done right, after just a few turns, the coconut will break open into two equal halves.
4 With the knife, cut "V"s into the flesh to facilitate removal of triangular chunks. Cut through the meat all the way to the shell, and then pry a bit to pop the chunks out. Sometimes it's possible to get underneath the meat with a spoon and pry away from the shell progressively.
5 Slice off remaining skin on the coconut meat with the knife. Cut into manageable chunks for use.

Chapter 2
Appetizers

Everyone loves to nibble on appetizers, either while cooking or when friends and family are around to enjoy a little conversation before the meal. But I would argue that few peoples love their appetizers more than those who live on the shores of the Mediterranean Sea, where little dishes, whether they go by the name tapas or *meze*, can be enjoyed for hours before the main meal. In Central Asia, little nibbles in the form of street foods calm the hunger pangs of folks on the go. These small meals are often so delicious you could serve them as a prelude to a fancy dinner.

In the Jewish community that my family was part of, most people observed the Sabbath in the traditional way, which meant they did not cook. There were always cold plates available for Saturday drop-ins. This tradition continued when they immigrated to New York. As guests would arrive at our home before the Friday night Sabbath eve meal, my mother would arrange cold appetizers on the coffee table in the living room. These would be transferred to the dinner table and kept on as side dishes. These appetizers lived up to their name; they awakened the appetite with their pungent spices.

All along the Silk Road, you'll find all kinds of nibbles that can easily be adapted to fit the Western definition of an appetizer. In this chapter, you'll find some of my favorites.

Bukharian Vegan Chopped Liver v GF

PECHONKHA

Chopped liver was a popular spread in my parents' home, made by sautéing liver, onions, and eggs. Truthfully, the smell made me nauseous and I could not understand why anyone would eat it. Subsequently, my mother turned my disgust to delight with this vegan chopped liver, which is made by combining dry roasted walnuts and sautéed onions with zucchini. She served it with pita slices. The high iron content from the walnuts is just as nutritious as chopped liver, but this version is low in fat. It is best eaten cold or at room temperature. Dip with your favorite vegetable or pita slices. For an even richer taste, top with a dash of walnut oil.

Prep Time: 7 minutes
Cook Time: 30 minutes
Makes 2 cups (500 g)

INGREDIENTS

¾ cup (75 g) shelled walnuts

2 tablespoons olive oil

1 onion, coarsely chopped

2 zucchini, trimmed and cut into ¼-in (6-mm) slices

¼ teaspoon salt

2 tablespoons unsalted tomato paste (page 42)

1 teaspoon ground cumin

1 tablespoon walnut oil, for garnish

1 Toast the walnuts in a large skillet over high heat, for about 2 minutes, or until they begin to brown a bit. Reduce the heat to medium and cook for about 7 minutes, or until dark brown on all sides stirring constantly and shaking the pan to prevent burning. Remove from the heat and pour onto a large plate or baking pan to cool completely.

2 In the same pan, heat the olive oil over medium-high heat. Add the onion and sauté, stirring and shaking the pan, for 10 minutes, or until it browns and caramelizes. Stir in the zucchini, season with salt and continue to sauté for 10 minutes, or until the zucchini browns a bit. Once cooked, remove from the heat and allow it to cool completely.

3 Place the zucchini and onion mixture, walnuts, tomato paste, and cumin into food processor or blender and pulse until smooth.

4 Pour into a medium-size bowl. Taste and season with additional salt if necessary. Drizzle a little walnut oil over the top for a richer flavor.

"The high iron content from the walnuts is just as nutritious as chopped liver."

Chickpea Falafel v GF

At almost every other corner in Israel, Middle Eastern street vendors and kiosks are selling chickpea fritters. It has evolved into the national dish that is easy to grab and go, serve in a pita pocket with a dollop of hummus, a little chopped salad, and then drizzled with tahini. Falafel originated in Egypt as a fava bean concoction; later, the Yemeni immigrants to Israel transformed it, making chickpeas the foundation. These patties are moist on the inside and crispy on the outside with plenty of spice, green herbs, and garlic. Serve warm with the Bukharian Tomato Salad and drizzled with tahini.

Prep Time: 10 minutes, plus 12 hours for soaking beans and 1 hour for the cooked beans in the refrigerator
Cook Time: 25 minutes, plus 45 minutes for cooking the beans
Makes 40 fritters

INGREDIENTS

2½ cups (500 g) dried chickpeas

1 onion, chopped

6 cloves garlic

1 cup (25 g) chopped fresh parsley

2 teaspoons ground coriander

2 teaspoons ground cumin

½ teaspoon red pepper flakes

1½ teaspoons salt

½ teaspoon freshly ground black pepper

Grapeseed oil, for frying

Sesame Seed Paste (tahini—page 42), for serving

Hummus (page 41), for serving

Bukharian Tomato Salad (page 95), for serving

1 Soak and skin the chickpeas according to the directions on page 29. Put the chickpeas into a food processor fitted with a metal blade. Add the onions, garlic, parsley, coriander, cumin, red pepper flakes, salt, and black pepper. Pulse until you have a thick batter. You do not want to liquefy this, or it will be difficult to form into patties. Refrigerate the mixture for at least 1 hour to thicken it even more.

2 When you are ready to cook, set a large skillet over medium-high heat, and add enough oil to come at least ½ in (1.25 cm) up the side of the pan. Carefully drop tablespoons of batter into the oil and fry for about 5 minutes on each side, or until golden. Use a wire mesh spider skimmer and transfer the falafel to paper towels to drain.

3 Place 2 or 3 falafels on a plate. Spoon in a dollop of hummus and some tomato salad and drizzle with tahini. Serve hot.

Mediterranean Chickpea Salad v GF

This Middle Eastern treat is a popular offering on the region's *meze* plates. *Meze* is a wonderful custom of serving a collage of little nibbles as a pre-dinner snack with drinks. This chickpea-based concoction relies on dill for freshness, onion for zest, and a sprinkling of lemon juice for tang. The creamy richness of the chickpeas balances perfectly with the lively dressing. The dressing has just the right ratio of lemon juice, olive oil, and salt to cling lightly to the chickpeas. The flavors blend even better if you marinate the salad for a few hours in the fridge before serving.

Prep Time: 10 minutes, plus 12 hours for soaking the beans
Cook Time: 45 minutes for the beans
Serves 4

INGREDIENTS

¾ cup (175 g) dried chickpeas or one 15-oz (425-g) can cooked chickpeas, drained

1 carrot, grated

1 stalk celery, grated

½ red onion, grated

½ green, red or yellow bell pepper, seeded, pith removed, and finely diced

3 tablespoons finely chopped fresh dill

3 tablespoons extra-virgin olive oil

Freshly squeezed juice of 1 lemon

¼ teaspoon salt

¼ teaspoon sugar

1 If you are using dried chickpeas, soak, skin and cook them according to the directions on page 29.

2 Combine the chickpeas, carrot, celery, onion, bell pepper, dill, olive oil, lemon juice, salt, and sugar in a medium-size bowl. Toss all the ingredients together, cover and refrigerate for at least an hour to allow all the flavors to meld. Serve at room temperature.

Stuffed Grape Leaves V GF

DOLMA

Along the Silk Road, almost every country has its own version of this favorite. As you get closer to the Mediterranean, stuffed grape leaves are found as a starter and can be eaten warm or cold. They bear delicious testimony to the fact that ingenious cooks have often found ways to make a delicacy from something that would otherwise be discarded. In this case, vineyards have been scattered throughout the region for literally thousands of years, producing a by-product of grape leaves that just begged to be put to use. Stuffing them with rice and herbs simmered in a lemony sauce makes for a wonderful finger food to be served on special occasions. The addition of beets and carrots to the stuffing naturally sweetens the grape leaves with pure ingredients alone. Although this can be a little time-consuming to make, when your hands join with the ingredients as you prepare this dish, know that you are conveying a life force. I suggest making these when you want to relax in the silent, rhythmic, sensual pleasure of making a luscious dish. They'll keep, covered, in the refrigerator for up to a week.

Prep Time: 45 minutes, plus 4 hours for soaking rice
Cook Time: 2 hours
Makes 35 rolls

INGREDIENTS

One 1-lb (500-g) jar grape leaves, or 50 fresh grape leaves

Stuffing

1 cup (200 g) short-grain brown rice

2 tablespoons olive oil

2 onions, minced

2 cloves garlic, minced

1 teaspoon salt

½ cup (125 ml) water

2 carrots, grated in a food processor

1 beet, peeled and grated in a food processor

1 stalk celery, grated in a food processor

½ cup (25 g) finely chopped fresh parsley

½ cup (25 g) finely chopped fresh mint

½ cup (25 g) finely chopped fresh dill

Freshly squeezed juice of 1 lemon

Sauce

1½ cups (375 ml) water

Freshly squeezed juice of 2 lemons

2 tablespoons extra-virgin olive oil

1 tablespoon sugar

1 teaspoon salt

1. Rinse and soak the rice according to the instructions on page 32.
2. If you are using preserved leaves, unroll them, rinse under cold water, and then soak in cold water for 15 minutes. If you are using fresh grape leaves, blanch them in lightly salted boiling water, for 5 minutes. Drain and pat dry, and then carefully cut off the stems.
3. To make the stuffing: Heat the oil in a large, heavy saucepan over medium heat. Sauté the onions, shaking and stirring the pan, for about 5 minutes, or until translucent. Add the garlic and cook for another 3 minutes, shaking and stirring the pan occasionally.
4. Pour in the rice and stir for about 5 minutes, or until opaque. Stir in the salt and the water, reduce the heat to low and simmer, covered, for 10 to 15 minutes, or until all the water is absorbed.
5. Remove the lid and add the carrots, beets, celery, parsley, mint, and dill. Let cool.
6. To assemble: Place a nice whole leaf on a work surface with the vein-side-up and

stem-side closest to you. Place 1 tablespoon of stuffing about ½ in (1.25 cm) from the stem end. Starting at that end, carefully fold the leaf over the stuffing and fold once to make a bundle. Then fold in the sides and roll up the remaining leaf into a neat package. Repeat to make 35 packages.
7. Cover the bottom of the saucepan with any torn leaves or 10 grape leaves. Arrange the rolls seam-side-down in layers.
8. To make the sauce: Whisk the water, lemon juice, oil, sugar, and salt in a medium bowl. Pour over the stuffed grape leaves. Put a heavy plate on top of the stuffed grape leaves to hold them down as they cook. Bring the stuffed grape leaves to a boil and then reduce the heat to low and simmer, covered, for 1 hour to 1 hour and 15 minutes, or until the rice is fully cooked. Once cooled, refrigerate for a day so the flavors can marry. When serving, arrange on a large platter and garnish with lemon wedges. Serve at room temperature or chilled.

Persian Green Frittata GF DF

KOOKOO SABZI

This Persian frittata dish was a staple in my mother's house whether we went out to the movies or on a flight somewhere across the Atlantic. It was easy to prepare, quick to bake and could be eaten hot or cold. My mother never bought food from a vendor and insisted that she could do it better and more healthfully. She was not wrong. Years ago, when I attempted to write the recipe for this dish, I noticed that my mother just grabbed anything green from her fridge. She did not measure, but just chopped away methodically like Edward Scissorhands at the parsley, leeks, spinach, dill, and coriander leaves. Her cutting away at this chlorophyll garden, rich in antioxidants, transported me to a green heaven, and still does. I have added potato to this frittata, to give it a bit more substance, which is especially welcome in the winter months when you are craving some starch. Clean and wash the vegetables thoroughly. Chopping the greens by hand is the traditional way, and it prevents the vegetables from turning mushy. Interestingly, this is the most traditional dish served on the day of Nowruz, the Persian New Year, which takes place in the spring. It is cooked in a round pan symbolizing a new beginning, and cut into wedges.

"This is the most traditional dish served on the day of the Persian New Year."

Prep Time: 15 minutes
Cook Time: 2 hours
Serves 12

INGREDIENTS

1 large potato

3 leeks

6 large eggs

2 cups (120 g) stemmed, washed and chopped fresh spinach

2 cups (50 g) chopped fresh parsley

1 cup (25 g) chopped fresh dill

1 cup (25 g) chopped fresh coriander leaves (cilantro)

1 teaspoon ground turmeric

1 teaspoon salt

½ teaspoon freshly ground black pepper

1 tablespoon rice flour

5 tablespoons olive oil (divided use)

1　Preheat the oven to 375°F (190°C). Scrub the potato, pierce it with a fork and bake for 45 minutes to 1 hour, or until it is soft enough to be mashed.

2　Prepare the leeks, which absorb large amounts of sand as they grow: Trim and discard the tough dark green outer leaves. Slice the leek lengthwise but leave the root intact. Hold it by the root to wash under cold running water. Separate the layers to get all the dirt out. When you are done, cut off and discard the root and chop the leeks.

3　Beat the eggs well in a large mixing bowl with a whisk. Then add the spinach, parsley, dill, coriander leaves, mashed potato, turmeric, salt, pepper, and flour. Mix thoroughly until well blended, add 1 tablespoon of the oil and stir well.

4　Heat the remaining 4 tablespoons of oil in a skillet set over medium heat and pour the mixture into the pan. Cover and cook for 20 minutes. Check by inserting a spatula under the frittata to see that it's cooked. The frittata should be browned and firm and should not fall apart.

5　With the spatula, slice the frittata into quarters to make it easier to turn and turn each quarter gently to the other side. If the frittata is still too soft and falls apart, cover the pan and cook for 5 more minutes before turning. Once you have turned it, cook for an additional 20 to 25 minutes, or until the entire frittata is cooked throughout.

6　Let it cool for a few minutes before further slicing. Place on a serving platter and serve hot or cold. Or pack it and take it with you as a meal on the go.

Turkish Leek Patties GF DF

KEFTES DE PRASSA

Leeks originated in Egypt and traveled to the Ottoman Empire, becoming part of this traditional patty eaten by Jews on special holidays. It's a variation on the Eastern European Jews' potato latke, which is traditionally eaten on Chanukah; the Sephardi Jews eat this as their Chanukah treat, since it, too, is fried in oil. Not much more than sautéed leeks (sautéing intensifies the flavor), potatoes and eggs create this deceptively delicious and addictive pancake. You must eat these when they are just cooked; otherwise they lose their perfect crispiness.

Prep Time: 20 minutes
Cook Time: 1 hour, 15 minutes
Makes 24 patties

INGREDIENTS
2 lbs (1 kg) leeks (about 10)

2 tablespoons olive oil

1½ teaspoons salt, plus additional salt as needed for boiling the potatoes

3 large potatoes, peeled

5 cloves garlic

3 large eggs, lightly beaten

½ teaspoon freshly ground black pepper

Grapeseed oil, for frying

Lemon wedges, for garnish

1 Prepare the leeks, which absorb large amounts of sand as they grow: Trim and discard the tough dark green outer leaves. Slice the leek lengthwise but leave the root intact. Hold it by the root to wash under cold running water. Separate the layers to get all the dirt out. When you are done, cut off and discard the root and chop the leeks.

2 Heat the olive oil in a large skillet set over medium-high heat. Add the leeks and season with the salt. Sauté the leeks, stirring and shaking the pan, for 7 to 8 minutes, until quite wilted.

3 Place the potatoes in a separate saucepan and add enough water to cover them by 1 in (2.5 cm). Add 1 teaspoon of salt for each quart of water. Cover the pot and boil for about 35 to 45 minutes, or until tender.

4 Combine the leeks, cooked potatoes, garlic, eggs, and black pepper in a food processor fitted with a metal blade. Pulse to form a paste.

5 Use the same skillet that you used for the leeks and pour at least ½ in (1.25 cm) of oil into it. Set it over medium-high heat. When the oil is sizzling hot, carefully drop large dollops of leek mixture into it. Lower the heat to medium, so as not to brown too quickly. Cook for 5 minutes on each side, then remove and drain on paper towel and serve warm. Arrange on a large platter and garnish with lemon wedges.

Persian Cucumber Yogurt Dip GF

MAST-O-KHIAR

Mast-o-khiar is much like the well-known Greek tzatziki, although made using slightly different ingredients. This version combines the best of both flavors, creating a creamy, cool salad with a flirt of mint on your tongue. I usually make this salad when my CSA delivers the crispest cucumbers at the peak of summer. It will cool you down from the blistering heat. It's wonderful with grilled vegetables or served on the side with stewed vegetables.

Prep Time: 10 minutes, plus 30 minutes
for the cucumbers to stand
Serves 4

INGREDIENTS
1 English cucumber
1 cup (245 g) plain yogurt
3 cloves garlic, minced
1 tablespoon chopped fresh mint
Salt, to taste
Freshly ground black pepper, to taste
Fresh mint sprigs, for garnish

1 Peel the cucumber and cut it in half lengthwise. Use a spoon to scrape out and discard the seeds. Cut the cucumber halves crosswise into ¼-in (6-mm) slices. Sprinkle with salt and let stand for 30 minutes. Then blot dry.

2 Meanwhile, in a bowl, whisk together the yogurt, garlic, mint, salt, and pepper. Place the cucumber in a bowl, add the dressing and toss gently. Garnish with fresh mint sprigs.

Persian Spinach & Yogurt Dip GF

BORANI ESFANAJ

In Iran, *borani* is an appetizer made with yogurt and some type of vegetable. I love the simplicity of this dip, which is essentially made with just two main ingredients—spinach and yogurt. Persians love to use spinach in their cuisine, as it originated in Central Asia. The popularity of yogurt in Persian cuisine, owes to the fact that for centuries there were abundant herds of sheep and lamb in the area, providing milk. In the days before advanced refrigeration, yogurt kept better. Today, spinach is widely available from spring to fall—and it's such a healthful ingredient, with its antioxidant and cancer fighting benefits. Additionally, spinach is known to be a good source of iron, and also helps fight cardiovascular disease. Serve this dip on a hot day with some crackers for scooping. For a complete meal, serve this with Persian Green Frittata (page 58).

Prep Time: 15 minutes
Cook Time: 25 minutes
Serves 6 to 8

INGREDIENTS

1 tablespoon olive oil

1 large onion, thinly sliced

1 clove garlic, minced

Small pinch of saffron

1 tablespoon hot water

3 cups (120 g) stemmed, washed, and chopped fresh spinach

2 cups (500 g) plain yogurt (thick is better)

Salt, to taste

Freshly ground black pepper, to taste

1 Heat the oil in a large skillet over medium high heat and sauté the onions, stirring and shaking the pan, for 15 minutes, or until they are soft and begin to color. Stir in the garlic and sauté for 1 minute, or until fragrant.

2 Steep the saffron in a small bowl with hot water, and let it sit until the water is tinted.

3 Add the spinach to the skillet and sauté for 5 minutes, or until wilted. Add the saffron water and stir to combine. Remove from the heat and cool completely. Fold in the yogurt, season with salt and pepper and refrigerate for several hours to allow the flavors to meld.

Italian Zucchini Fritters GF

During the summer when there is an abundance of zucchini, this is a great recipe that makes quick work of the bounty. These crispy, warm fritters are soft and moist on the inside and contrast nicely with the sharp flavor of Parmesan cheese. This is one of those dishes that cross-references with others from neighboring countries. You can find similar dishes in North Africa and throughout the Mediterranean region. That's no wonder, since many Jews fled from the Spanish Inquisition to Greece, Syria, and Italy. In Syria this appetizer with its regional variation is known as *kusa b'jibn*, while in Greece this is made with feta cheese and known as *kolokithokeftedes*. I learned of these fritters while visiting with my aunts and uncles who migrated to Milan from Afghanistan. To add a delicate Indian piquancy, I suggest dipping the fritters into the Mango Chutney—which seamlessly blends the far ends of the Silk Road.

Prep Time: 20 minutes
Cook Time: 20 minutes
Makes 12 fritters

INGREDIENTS

3 zucchini, grated

⅔ cup (40 g) freshly grated
   Parmesan cheese

2 large eggs, beaten

4 tablespoons all-purpose
   gluten-free flour

Salt, to taste

Freshly ground black
   pepper, to taste

Grapeseed oil, for frying

Mango Chutney (page 48),
   for serving

1 Squeeze the zucchini in a dish towel to remove any excess water. Then combine with Parmesan cheese, eggs, and flour, and season with salt and pepper.

2 Heat enough oil to cover the base of a large frying pan. Carefully spoon about 2 tablespoons of the mixture into the oil to make each fritter, cooking 3 to 4 fritters at a time. Cook for 3 to 5 minutes, turn and cook for 3 to 5 minutes on the other side, or until golden. Drain on paper towels and serve warm with a dollop of chutney.

Indian Red Lentil Falafel v GF

VADAS

You have probably heard of falafel made from chickpeas, but have you heard of falafel made from red lentils? Throughout India, red lentil falafel is a fast-food item available at railway stations and from street vendors. Crunchy on the outside and chewy on the inside, most of its flavoring comes from the spices. I usually whip up a batch in the winter when seasonal produce is in short supply. Legumes of all kinds are an ideal dish during the colder months because they keep for a long time. Usually lentils need not be soaked, as they cook quickly. In this dish they are combined with the other ingredients to make a batter before they are cooked, so I do soak them. (Be sure to allow enough time for soaking!) Eat it like the Indians do—with your hands. There is something so primal and freeing when you are not using utensils; you get the full sensory experience of eating. Accompany with *raita* dipping sauce or chutney for a fast and fun meal.

Roasted Eggplant Paté v GF

BAUNJON

Prep Time: 10 minutes, plus 2 hours for
  soaking the lentils
Cook Time: 20 minutes
Makes 20 pieces

INGREDIENTS

1 cup (200 g) dried red lentils, picked
  through for stones and debris

1 small onion

3 cloves garlic

4 tablespoons fresh coriander leaves
  (cilantro)

1 small green chili, seeded and minced

1 teaspoon minced fresh ginger

¾ teaspoon salt

½ teaspoon ground cumin

Grapeseed oil, for frying

Mango Chutney (page 48) or Raita
  (page 43), for serving

1 Wash the lentils in a bowl of cold water and keep changing the water until
it runs clear. (This is very important
or the lentils will get scummy.) Soak
the lentils in fresh water for at least 2
hours. Drain and pat dry.

2 Process the lentils, onion, garlic, fresh
coriander leaves, chili, ginger, salt,
and cumin in a food processor until
thoroughly combined.

3 Pour at least ½ in (1.25 cm) of oil into
a large skillet and set it over medium-
high heat. Carefully drop the batter, 1
tablespoon at a time, into the oil, being
careful not to crowd the pan, and fry
for about 5 minutes on each side, or
until golden. Work in batches if necessary. Use a wire mesh spider skimmer
to transfer to paper towels to drain.
Serve warm with the chutney or *raita*.

Every country along the Silk Route has
its own version of this eggplant paté.
I grew up on the Bukharian version,
which, unlike others, is flavored very
simply, with garlic and salt. It was a
staple starter dish at our Friday night
Sabbath dinners. Typically, we would
spread this paté on challah bread
after we recited the blessings to start
the Friday night meal. Broiling the
eggplant imparts a pleasingly subtle,
smoky flavor that eliminates the need
for lots of other seasoning. This also
makes a wonderfully delicious, low-fat
spread for sandwiches or is great with
vegetable crudités. It will keep in the
fridge, in a covered glass container, for
up to 1 week.

Prep Time: 7 minutes
Cook Time: 35 minutes
Makes 1 to 1½ cups (250 to 350 g)

INGREDIENTS

2 eggplants

3 cloves garlic, smashed

½ teaspoon salt

1 Preheat the broiler. Cut several slits in the
eggplant and roast them directly on the
oven rack, 6 in (15 cm) away from the
heat source, for 30 to 35 minutes, or until
very tender.

2 Let stand, and when they are cool enough
to handle, remove the skin with a fork, using a gliding motion and making sure not
to leave any skin behind.

3 Coarsely chop the eggplant in a medium-
size bowl. Combine with the garlic and
salt until the paté is thoroughly mixed.

Chapter 3
Soups

The soups eaten along the Silk Road are typically redolent of aromatic, zesty spices. These soups fall into two categories: those that are made with broths left over from other dishes and enriched with vegetables and herbs (there was no waste on the Silk Road—all leftovers were used in some way), and those that are hearty enough to be a meal on their own.

I love soup, and the ones that I have included in this chapter are classic Silk Road pottages, as well as several inspired by Silk Road seasonings and style. Many of these soups will make a lovely first course, while others will serve as filling, nourishing meals in their own right. Some soups require minimal work, and many entail only chopping the ingredients, and an occasional stir.

It's not a bad idea to enjoy your meals in a variety of ways—to keep yourself from getting stuck with the same old boring dishes. When you are in a hurry, nothing beats a bowl of soup that has a concentrated amount of nutrition in one serving. It's easy to make, keeps well, is simple to reheat, freezes nicely, it's filling—and it tastes so good!

Lentil Tomato Soup V GF

HARIRA

A famous Moroccan tomato-based soup, *harira* is seasoned with fragrant ginger, cinnamon, robust coriander leaves, and parsley. Moroccans love *harira* best during the month of Ramadan, when it's frequently served to break the fast at sunset. What is so interesting about this soup, as well as many other dishes found along the Silk Road, is that it is akin to the sweet soup prepared by North Indian and Pakistani families, who call it by a similar name, *hareera*. *Hareera* is typically consumed during the winter rainy season, when a filling, warm dish is desired. I love the way all the countries along the Silk Road have influenced each other. This particular version of *harira* is based on the one made by my mother-in-law, Shirley Klein, who lives in Durban, South Africa. She adapted it from her Muslim neighbors. I removed the small amount of meat that characterizes most *harira* recipes and made it a vegetarian dish. The final touch, a squeeze of lemon juice, gives it a little zing.

Prep Time: 30 minutes, plus 12 hours for soaking the beans and 4 hours for soaking the rice
Cook Time: 2 hours, plus 45 minutes for cooking the beans
Serves 8 to 10

INGREDIENTS

1 cup (200 g) dried chickpeas or one 15-oz (425-g) can cooked chickpeas

1 cup (200 g) dried brown lentils, rinsed and picked through for stones and debris or one 15-oz (425-g) can lentils

½ cup (125 g) short-grain brown rice

2 tablespoons olive oil

2 stalks celery, diced

1 onion, diced

One 1-in (2.5-cm) piece of fresh ginger, peeled and minced (about 1 tablespoon)

1 teaspoon ground cinnamon

1 teaspoon paprika

2¼ cups (565 ml) Vegetable Broth (page 45)

4 tomatoes, puréed in a food processor, or one 15-oz (425-g) can puréed tomatoes

½ cup (15 g) finely chopped fresh parsley

¾ cup (20 g) finely chopped fresh coriander leaves (cilantro)

Pinch of saffron

Salt, to taste

Freshly ground black pepper, to taste

Fresh coriander sprigs (cilantro), for garnish

2 lemons, quartered, for garnish

Moroccans love this soup best during the month of Ramadan."

1. If you are using dried chickpeas, then you'll need to soak, skin, and cook them according to the instructions on page 29.
2. Cook the lentils according to the instructions on page 28.
3. Rinse the rice in a strainer under cold running water for 30 seconds, swirling the rice around with your hand.
4. Heat the oil in a large saucepan set over medium-high heat. Sauté the celery and onions, stirring and shaking the pan frequently, for about 7 minutes, or until translucent.
5. Add the ginger, cinnamon, and paprika and continue stirring for about a minute, or until fragrant.
6. Pour the broth, tomatoes and rice into a saucepan and cook over medium-high heat until boiling. Once the mixture boils, reduce the heat and simmer, covered, for 20 minutes.
7. Add the chickpeas and lentils; increase the heat and bring to a boil again. When the mixture boils, reduce the heat to low and simmer, covered, for 1 hour. During the hour, check the soup to make sure nothing is sticking to the bottom; scrape with a wooden spoon if necessary. If the soup is too thick, add water, about 4 tablespoons at a time.
8. When the soup is done, stir in the parsley and chopped coriander leaves with a few threads of saffron. Season to taste with salt and pepper. The soup should be thick and rich. Ladle the soup into bowls and garnish with the remaining coriander sprigs. Garnish with lemon wedges and by all means squeeze some lemon into your soup for a fresh tartness.

Persian Bean & Noodle Soup v GF

ASH-E RESHTEH

For the Persian New Year, Nowruz, this traditional soup is always served. Noodles are believed to bring good fortune, and it is customary to serve *ash-e reshteh* or any noodles before embarking on something new. The noodles symbolize the threads of life, and are associated with change and new beginnings. *Ash-e reshteh* has traveled westward where it has morphed into the Moroccan *harira*, with its mix of legumes, but unlike *harira*, *Ash-e reshteh* is based on a green-herbed stew. This soup thickens when cooled, so add ¼ cup (65 ml) or more of boiling water as needed when reheating.

Prep Time: 30 minutes, plus 12 hours for soaking the beans
Cook Time: 2 hours, 20 minutes
Serves 12 to 15

INGREDIENTS

4 tablespoons dried red kidney beans

4 tablespoons dried navy beans

4 tablespoons dried chickpeas

½ lb (500 g) brown rice spaghetti pasta (available in natural food stores)

4 tablespoons oil

4 onions, peeled and thinly sliced

4 teaspoons salt

1 teaspoon freshly ground black pepper

1 teaspoon ground turmeric

12 cups (2.75 liters) water

½ cup (100 g) lentils, rinsed and picked through for stones and debris

1 tablespoon rice flour

2 cups (120 g) chopped spinach (fresh or frozen)

1 cup (50 g) coarsely chopped fresh parsley

¾ cup (75 g) trimmed and sliced green onions (scallions)

½ cup (25 g) finely chopped fresh dill

Topping (optional)

2 tablespoons oil

1 large onion, peeled and thinly sliced

1 tablespoon dried mint

1 cup (245 g) plain yogurt

1 Soak the kidney beans, navy beans, and chickpeas in separate containers, according to the instructions on pages 28 and 29. When the beans are soaked, drain and skin the chickpeas.

2 Cook the rice pasta according to package directions, and then set aside.

3 When you are ready to cook, heat the oil in a large stockpot set over medium heat. Add the onions and sauté, stirring occasionally, for 10 minutes, or until translucent. Add the salt, pepper, and turmeric.

4 Stir in the kidney beans, navy beans, and chickpeas and sauté for a minute. Pour in the water and bring to a boil, then cover and simmer for 45 minutes over medium heat.

5 Add the lentils and cook for 20 minutes longer.

6 Then, add the rice flour and stir occasionally for 10 minutes.

7 Add the spinach, parsley, green onions, and dill and continue to cook, stirring from time to time for 30 minutes. Add the cooked rice pasta. If the soup is too thick, add ½ cup (125 ml) water at a time and return to a boil. Reduce the heat to low, cover and keep warm.

8 To make the topping, heat the oil in a skillet set over medium-high heat and sauté the onions, stirring, for about 15 minutes, or until they are browned. Add in the mint and stir until fragrant. Pour the soup into a large serving bowls and scatter the fried onion over the tops. Drizzle with yogurt and serve.

"Noodles symbolize the threads of life, and are associated with change and new beginnings."

Pumpkin Soup V GF

Pumpkins are wonderful because they keep for months and are an ideal source of nutrition when other vegetables are out of season. Pumpkin is ideal for soups, because when cooked, much of it breaks down to give the dish a lovely, creamy texture. The addition of ginger and cinnamon give the earthy pumpkin a more full-bodied flavor. The maple syrup complements the pumpkin and serves as a testament to my family's journey from the Silk Road all the way to America. Sugar pumpkins are ideal for this recipe. Buy one that is about 2 lbs (1 kg), because you will discard the peel.

Prep Time: 25 minutes
Cook Time: 1 hour, 10 minutes,
   plus 10 minutes for roasting the nuts
Serves 10

INGREDIENTS

4 tablespoons oil

2 large onions, diced

One 1-in (2.5-cm) piece of fresh ginger, peeled and coarsely chopped (about 1 tablespoon)

7 cups (1.75 liters) Vegetable Broth (page 45)

One 2-lb (1-kg) sugar pumpkin, peeled, seeded and cubed or one 15-oz (425-g) can unseasoned pumpkin purée

2 sweet potatoes, peeled and cubed

1 white potato, peeled and cubed

½ cup (50 g) Applesauce (page 46)

3 tablespoons pure maple syrup

1 teaspoon ground cinnamon

1 tablespoon salt

¼ teaspoon white pepper

½ cup (125 ml) Coconut Milk (page 49)

Roasted pine nuts, for garnish (See Oven Roasted Nuts, page 44)

1   Heat the oil in a large saucepan set over medium-high heat. Sauté the onions, stirring and shaking the pan frequently, for about 10 minutes, or until golden.

Then stir in the ginger and cook for an additional 3 minutes.

2   Pour in the broth, and add the pumpkin, sweet potatoes, white potato, and applesauce. Bring to a boil. Cover, reduce the heat to low and simmer for 35 minutes, or until fully cooked.

3   Purée the vegetables until smooth with an immersion blender.

4   Add the syrup, cinnamon, salt, and pepper and continue simmering for an additional 10 minutes.

5   Stir in the coconut milk and remove from the heat. Ladle into bowls and garnish with pine nuts, if you wish.

CUTTING UP PUMPKINS

Using your biggest, heaviest chef's knife, insert the point at the top of the pumpkin and slowly and carefully push it in, applying pressure straight down, and pausing to wiggle the knife from side to side, widening the crack. Work your way slowly down the side of the pumpkin. Repeat on the other side. Push straight down through the second crack and split through the bottom of the pumpkin, cutting until the two halves are attached only at the stem. Pull the halves apart with your hands, cracking at the stem.

Lentil & Carrot Soup v GF

The cumin-laced steam rising from this bowl of orange velvet clears my head. The red pepper flakes add some heat to the furnace and make you take notice. The backbone of this soup is the lentil, the most revered legume in biblical times, especially in the Jewish religion, in which lentils were eaten during mourning, symbolizing the circle of life. Lentils were part of the staple diet along the Spice Route. It's easy to see why; they're fast and easy to prepare, especially on a blustery winter day when your body needs instant warmth and comfort food. Heating the spices in a dry pan before you begin to cook releases their essential oils and creates marvelous flavor and aroma. In India, this is called tempering the spices. As an option, serve this with a dollop of plain yogurt on top, and warm *naan* bread on the side. When reheating this soup, dilute with some water or broth if it's too thick.

Prep Time: 10 minutes
Cook Time: 30 minutes
Serves 4 to 6

INGREDIENTS

1 cup (200 g) dried red lentils, picked through for stones and debris 2 teaspoons cumin seeds

½ teaspoon red pepper flakes

2 tablespoons coconut oil

3 cups (150 g) grated carrots

4 cups (1 liter) Vegetable Broth (page 45)

1 teaspoon salt

1 Wash the lentils in a bowl of cold water and keep changing the water until it runs clear. (This is very important or the lentils will get scummy.)

2 Heat a large saucepan over medium heat and dry-fry the cumin seeds and red pepper flakes for 1 minute, or until they start to jump around the pan and become fragrant. Watch them carefully and remove from the heat before they burn.

3 With a spoon, transfer about half of the spice mixture from the pan to a small bowl and set aside for later.

4 Add the oil, carrots, lentils, and broth to the spices in the pan and bring to a boil. Simmer, covered, for about 20 minutes, or until the lentils are softened.

5 Season with the salt and sprinkle with reserved spice mixture. Ladle into bowls and serve.

Split Pea Soup v GF

This is a variation on an ancient soup that originated in Greece and Italy. It eventually came to the United States, where it was reborn with the addition of ham. Today, it's the perfect soup for winter, when local vegetables are not readily available. Packed with protein from the split peas, it's hearty and satisfying. I just love the way the peas break down and naturally thicken the soup, and the bits of carrot and celery add flavor and texture. In lieu of ham, the cumin smokes up the soup with an Indian flair. The coconut oil, which comes in solid form and must be melted, gives it a nutty flavor. When reheating this soup, you may need to add some water if it's too thick. Add in increments of 4 tablespoons at a time.

Prep Time: 15 minutes
Cook Time: 1 hour, 10 minutes
Serves 4 to 6

INGREDIENTS

2 tablespoons extra-virgin coconut oil (available in natural foods supermarkets and specialty stores)

1 tablespoon curry powder

1 teaspoon ground cumin

1 large onion, chopped

3 cloves garlic, chopped

½ teaspoon red pepper flakes

Gingered Sweet Potato Soup V GF

An exotic blend of creamy sweet potatoes with a kick of hot sauce and some coconut milk to mellow it all out. It's a delicious soup that uses fall produce, so when we eat it, we're in harmony with the natural cycles of our environment. Thanks to my sister-in-law, Janine Solarsh, for sharing this recipe with me, all the way from South Africa.

2 large carrots, chopped

2 stalks celery, chopped

5½ cups (1.25 liters) Vegetable Broth (page 45)

1½ cups (350 g) green split peas, rinsed and picked through for stones and debris

½ teaspoon salt

1 teaspoon toasted cumin seeds (see Toasted Seeds and Spices, page 44), for garnish

1 Melt the coconut oil in a large soup pot over medium-high heat. Then add the curry powder and ground cumin and sauté, stirring and shaking the pan frequently, until it sizzles and is fragrant.

2 Add the onion, garlic and red pepper flakes, stirring often for about 7 minutes, or until the onions are translucent.

3 Stir in the carrots and celery and cook for about 5 minutes, or until the celery starts to turn translucent. Add the broth and split peas. Bring to a boil, then simmer, covered, for about 50 minutes, or until the split peas are tender. Season with salt.

4 When you are ready to serve, ladle the soup into bowls and garnish with toasted cumin seeds.

Prep Time: 20 minutes
Cook Time: 1 hour
Serves 10

INGREDIENTS

3 tablespoons oil

2 onions, finely chopped

3 cloves garlic, finely chopped

One 1-in (2.5-cm) piece of fresh ginger, peeled and grated (about 1 tablespoon)

3 sweet potatoes, peeled and cubed

1 white potato, peeled and cubed

½ cup (125 ml) water

3½ cups (875 ml) Vegetable Broth (page 45)

1 cup (250 ml) Coconut Milk (page 49)

1 teaspoon North African Chili Paste (*harissa*—page 43, or available in Middle Eastern markets and specialty stores)

Salt, to taste

3 tablespoons finely chopped fresh coriander leaves (cilantro), for garnish

1 Heat the oil in a large saucepan set over medium-high heat. Sauté the onions, garlic and ginger for about 7 minutes, or until the onions are translucent.

2 Stir in the sweet potatoes and white potato with the water. Let the potatoes sweat gently for 15 minutes, stirring occasionally, until slightly softened.

3 Pour in the broth and bring to a boil. Reduce the heat and simmer, covered, for 25 minutes, or until the potatoes are thoroughly soft. Pour in the coconut milk and chili paste and stir to combine.

4 Once the soup has cooled, use an immersion blender to process the mixture until smooth. Season with salt to taste. Ladle the soup into bowls and garnish with coriander leaves.

Sweet Potato & Lentil Soup v GF

The most revered legume in biblical times was the lentil, especially in the Jewish religion where lentils were eaten during mourning, symbolizing the circle of life. Preparing this soup transports me to my biblical and ancestral roots. Lentils were part of the staple diet along the Spice Route, a region also well known for its curry blends. Combining an ancient legume from the East with the orange-fleshed sweet potato creates a thick and hearty soup packed with spicy flavor.

Prep Time: 20 minutes
Cook Time: 1 hour, 10 minutes
Serves 8 to 10

INGREDIENTS

2 tablespoons oil

1 large onion, chopped

4 cloves garlic, minced

2 sweet potatoes, peeled and cut into ½-in (1.25-cm) cubes

2 large stalks celery, chopped

1 tablespoon curry powder

One 1-in (2.5-cm) piece of fresh ginger, peeled and grated (about 1 tablespoon)

1 teaspoon ground cumin

1 teaspoon ground coriander

⅛ teaspoon ground red pepper

2 quarts (1.75 liters) Vegetable Broth (page 45) or water

1 cup (200 g) dried lentils, rinsed and picked through for stones and debris

1 teaspoon salt

1 Heat the oil in a large saucepan over medium heat. Sauté the onions and garlic for a few minutes until the onions start to soften. Add the sweet potatoes and celery, and cook, stirring occasionally, for about 10 minutes, or until the sweet potatoes turn a bright orange.

2 Add the curry powder, ginger, cumin, ground coriander, and ground red pepper and cook, stirring, for 1 minute.

3 Pour in the vegetable broth or water and the lentils and heat to boiling over high heat. Reduce the heat to low. Cover and simmer, stirring occasionally, for 40 to 50 minutes, or until the lentils are tender. Add the salt to taste. Ladle into bowls and serve.

Spiced Red Lentil Soup v GF

There are many varieties of red lentil soup, which developed along the Silk Road. The Iraqis prepare theirs with rice and vegetables and a hefty dose of garlic. In North Africa, they add tomatoes. In Turkey, they add dried red peppers, wheatberries, mint, and green peppers, while the Syrians prepare this soup with coriander seeds and cumin. This South Indian version is prepared with sautéed red onions in a coconut-lime base that is cooked with red lentils, which naturally break down to give the soup its creamy texture. The perfectly balanced sweet, sour, and spicy flavor will wake up the sleepiest taste buds. This soup makes me feel like I'm soaking up sunshine; its warm orange hue seems to give off a vibrant energy. Enjoy it as a main meal with sticky rice, or on its own as a hearty, protein-packed dish. It freezes really well, but I'll doubt you will have any leftovers since it's so "moreish."

Prep Time: 15 minutes
Cook Time: 1 hour
Serves 6

INGREDIENTS

1 cup (200 g) small dried red lentils, picked through for stones and debris

2 tablespoons olive oil

2 red onions, finely chopped

4 cloves garlic, minced

1 bird's-eye chili pepper, seeded and finely chopped

One 1-in (2.5-cm) piece fresh lemongrass, outer leaves removed and inside finely sliced

1 teaspoon ground coriander

1 teaspoon paprika

1⅔ cups (325 ml) Coconut Milk (page 49)

3¾ cups (1 liter) water

1 cup (30 g) finely chopped fresh coriander leaves (cilantro)

3 green onions (scallions), green parts only, trimmed and sliced

2 tablespoons freshly squeezed lime juice

Salt, to taste

Freshly ground black pepper, to taste

1 Wash the lentils in a bowl of cold water and keep changing the water until it runs clear. (This is very important or the lentils will get scummy.)

2 Heat the oil in a large saucepan set over medium heat. Sauté the onion, garlic, chili, and lemongrass for about 8 minutes, or until the onions turn pink.

3 Add the lentils, ground coriander, and paprika. Stir in the coconut milk and water and bring to a boil. Cover, reduce the heat and simmer 40 to 45 minutes, or until lentils look mashed.

4 Add the coriander leaves and green onions, reserving a little of each for garnish. Pour in the lime juice and season with the salt and pepper to taste. Ladle into bowls and garnish with the reserved coriander leaves and green onions.

Yellow Split Pea Soup v GF

DAL

Dal is a Hindi word that refers to a preparation of *pulses* (dried lentils, peas or beans) that have been stripped of their outer hulls and split. It can also mean the thick stew beloved in Indian cuisine. Yellow split pea *dal* is a staple of Indian vegetarian cuisine. I love this recipe for many reasons, but most for my nostalgia for Morris. He was my Indian nanny when I was a child. We often had business guests from other lands and it was my mother's custom to prepare dishes of their national cuisines. When our guests were from Bombay, Morris taught my mother vegetarian dishes from his native country. I also love this soup for its simplicity and extraordinary blend of flavors. This dish is infused with the taste of Indian spices, onions, a whole bulb of garlic, lemon juice, and tomatoes, forming a citrusy delight. It's a fantastic way to prepare split peas and, for me, a way to honor Morris. This soup thickens when cooled, so add ¼ cup (65 ml) of boiling water or more as needed when reheating.

Prep Time: 20 minutes
Cook Time: 2 hours, 25 minutes
Serves 8 to 10

INGREDIENTS

1¾ cups (400 g) yellow split peas, rinsed and picked through for stones and debris

10 cups (2.25 liters) water

1 tablespoon oil

1 head garlic, minced

2 tablespoons mustard seeds

1 tablespoon cumin seeds

1 tablespoon curry powder

2 teaspoons ground turmeric

2 tomatoes, chopped

2 potatoes, diced into ¼-in (6-mm) cubes

2 carrots, diced into ¼-in (6-mm) cubes

1 onion, diced

Freshly squeezed juice of 2 lemons

Salt, to taste

Freshly ground black pepper, to taste

1 Bring the peas and 8 cups (1.75 liters) of water to a boil in a large saucepan set over high heat. Reduce the heat and simmer, covered, skimming the foam from the surface occasionally, for 40 minutes, or until the peas are somewhat tender. (Skimming eliminates some of the gaseous effects of the peas.)

2 Heat the oil in a large skillet and sauté the minced garlic, shaking and stirring the pan for about 30 seconds, or until the garlic begins to soften. You may need to reduce the heat to prevent the garlic from burning. Stir in the mustard seeds, cumin seeds, curry powder, and turmeric. Cook for 4 minutes, or until fragrant. Set aside.

3 Once the peas are cooked, add the remaining 2 cups (500 ml) water, the tomatoes, potatoes, carrots, and onion. Stir to combine and bring to boil. Then simmer, covered, for another 40 minutes.

4 Stir in the garlic mixture and lemon juice. If the soup is too thick, add water to thin it a bit. Season with salt and pepper. Simmer for another 5 minutes to blend the flavors, and then ladle the soup into bowls and serve.

> "This dish is infused with the taste of Indian spices—a citrusy delight."

Butternut Squash Soup v GF

When cooler weather overtakes the waning summer heat, call back the warmth with a classic autumn soup that envelopes the taste buds with the sweet, nuttiness of winter squash, a blend of harvest flavors—carrots, celery, and apples—and a tickle of curry powder and ginger. Don't skip the garnish of cashews (for a hearty crunch) and raisins (for chewy sweetness). The result: a complex and delicious fall soup.

Prep Time: 20 minutes
Cook Time: 40 minutes, plus 10 minutes for roasting the nuts
Serves 4 to 6

INGREDIENTS

1 tablespoon olive oil

1 onion, chopped

2 teaspoons curry powder

1 teaspoon ground ginger

One 2-in (5-cm) piece fresh ginger, peeled and minced (about 2 tablespoons)

2 stalks celery, chopped

2 carrots, chopped

3 to 4 lb (1.5 to 2 kg) butternut squash, peeled, seeded, and cubed

1 cooking apple such as McIntosh, peeled, cored, and chopped

3 cups (750 ml) Vegetable Broth (page 45)

Salt, to taste

Freshly ground black pepper, to taste

4 tablespoons halved roasted cashews (see Oven Roasted Nuts, page 44), for garnish

4 tablespoons raisins, for garnish

Curried Parsnip Soup V GF

1 Heat the oil in a large stockpot over medium-high heat. Sauté the onion, stirring and shaking the pan frequently for about 7 minutes, or until it is just starting to turn translucent. Add the curry powder and ground ginger. Stir for a minute to allow the flavors to blend. Then add the fresh ginger, celery, and carrots, and cook, stirring frequently, for 5 minutes.

2 Add the squash, apple and broth. Bring to a boil; then reduce the heat to low. Simmer, covered, for 15 minutes, or until the squash has softened.

3 Once cooled, purée the mixture in a food processor until thick and creamy. Season with salt and pepper to taste. Ladle into bowls and garnish with the cashews and raisins.

The months of frost bring parsnip season! Parsnips are native to the Silk Road region and have been eaten there since antiquity. When cooked, their buttery, slightly spicy, sweet flavor offers undertones of honey—with a subtle taste of cardamom. Combine this complex flavor profile with the aromatic bite of curry powder, ginger and a hint of cinnamon and you've got a soup that is perfect for those cold winter months.

Prep Time: 15 minutes
Cook Time: 50 minutes
Serves 6

INGREDIENTS

3 tablespoons coconut oil

1 large onion, chopped

One 2-in (5-cm) piece fresh ginger, peeled and minced (about 2 tablespoons)

2 teaspoons curry powder

1 teaspoon ground ginger

1 lb (500 g) parsnips (about 5 to 6), peeled and sliced

2 tablespoons sugar

2 teaspoons salt

6 cups (1.5 liters) water

½ teaspoon ground cinnamon

¼ teaspoon freshly ground black pepper

1 Heat the oil in a large saucepan over medium heat. Sauté the onion, stirring, for about 7 minutes, or until translucent. Add the ginger and stir for a minute. Then add the curry powder and ground ginger and sauté for a couple of minutes to release the flavors.

2 Add the parsnips and stir in the sugar. Reduce the heat to low, add the salt and let sweat, covered, for 15 minutes. Stir occasionally to make sure that the vegetables don't burn or stick to the pan. Pour in the water and continue to cook, covered, over low heat for an additional 15 minutes.

3 Remove from the heat and blend with an immersion blender. Season with cinnamon and pepper. Ladle into bowls and serve.

Chapter 4
Salads

Boldly colored beets and carrots, colorful assorted peppers and earthy mushrooms, strawberries, pumpkin seeds...there is really nothing that can't be thrown into a salad from your local produce market or CSA. Countless combinations of vegetables, grains, fruits, and herbs create superb salads, each with its own medley of contrasting colors, shapes, and textures. All of the salads presented here have this spunky characteristic inspired by the Silk Road.

Salads of the Silk Road typically accompany the main course and are seldom served separately. Just like appetizers, they are part of the meal, further blurring the distinction between salads and other sides. Most salads from the region are not the big leafy green salads to which you might be accustomed (these were introduced by the Romans in the early part of the Common Era). Most Silk Road salads consist of non-leafy greens, because, when grown naturally, leaves harbor insects that become bothersome to clean.

In most cases, these salads can be prepared ahead of time—often with a food processor if you are short on time—and stored in the fridge for a few days. You can even create an elaborate meal with just salads on the table.

Sesame Kale Salad v GF

Kale is a green powerhouse of nutrition, and this recipe, flavored with sesame dressing, is sure to sway anyone who isn't already a fan. I love to eat this with a side of Sesame Noodles (page 157) and tofu, which makes it a wonderful, wholesome meal that is low in fat, yet high in taste and antioxidants. You can eat this warm or cold. It will keep, covered, in the refrigerator for a few days, but I can assure you that you will not have any leftovers.

Prep Time: 10 minutes
Cook Time: 10 minutes
Serves 4 to 6

INGREDIENTS

1 lb (500 g) fresh kale, roughly chopped

Sesame Dressing

2 tablespoons soy sauce (gluten free)

2 tablespoons toasted sesame oil

1 tablespoon toasted sesame seeds (see Toasted Seeds and Spices, page 44)

1 clove garlic, smashed

2 tablespoons agave nectar

1 tablespoon apple cider vinegar

Dash of freshly ground black pepper or ground red pepper, to taste

1 Rinse the kale well in large bowl of cold water. Place it in colander to drain.

2 Discard any discolored leaves. To trim away tough stems, make a V-shaped cut at stem end, slicing around the tough spine. Stack the leaves and cut them into 3 to 4-in (7.5 to 10-cm) pieces.

3 Heat 4 tablespoons of water in a large pot set over medium-high heat. Add the kale and cook for 3 to 5 minutes, or until it wilts and is tender but not mushy, stirring occasionally. Let cool and the squeeze out as much water as possible from the kale. Transfer to a large bowl.

4 To make the dressing: in a jar with a lid, mix the soy sauce, sesame oil, sesame seeds, garlic, agave nectar, apple cider vinegar, and ground black pepper or ground red pepper. Cover tightly and shake until all the ingredients are thoroughly combined. Just before you are ready to serve, pour the dressing over the greens. Toss and serve.

Asian Coleslaw v GF

Travelers on the Silk Road journeyed to East Asia to trade in silks and other goods. If this crunchy cabbage salad had been around then, they might have put it on their shopping list. As nutty as it is tasty, it gets an Asian accent from the combination of sesame seeds, cabbage and the soy sauce in the dressing. It's a quick and easy salad to prepare and makes for a nice starter in an Asian meal. It can be made in advance and refrigerated for up to 24 hours; however if you do that, add the nuts and seeds just before serving to retain crunchiness.

Prep Time: 20 minutes, plus 30 minutes for marinating
Serves 8

INGREDIENTS

Salad

1 small green cabbage, cored and sliced into thin strips

2 carrots, trimmed and cut into thin matchsticks

4 green onions (scallions), green part only, thinly sliced

⅓ cup (40 g) toasted sesame seeds (see Toasted Seeds and Spices, page 44)

½ cup (65 g) shelled sunflower seeds, roasted

½ cup (35 g) slivered almonds

Dressing

¾ cup (175 ml) oil

⅓ cup (80 ml) agave nectar

½ cup (125 ml) red wine vinegar

2 tablespoons gluten-free soy sauce

1 Combine the cabbage, carrots, green onions, sesame seeds, sunflower seeds, and almonds in a large bowl and toss to combine.

2 To make the dressing: in a jar with a lid, combine the oil, agave nectar, vinegar, and soy sauce. Cover tightly and shake until all the ingredients are well mixed. Add the dressing to the slaw, mixing well. Cover with plastic wrap and refrigerate for at least 30 minutes before serving. (If you plan to make it any earlier, don't forget to keep the nuts and seeds out until just before you serve.)

Orange & Fennel Salad v GF

Fennel and oranges are a classic Mediterranean combination, and with good reason. The fennel, with its aromatic licorice flavor, pairs nicely with the tangy-sweetness of the oranges. A modern twist—sweetened dried cranberries—provides just the right accent of tartness. The juice that accumulates when you slice the oranges makes the dressing even more flavorful. The result: a cool, refreshing summer salad.

Prep Time: 15 minutes
Cook Time: 10 minutes for roasting the nuts
Serves 4

INGREDIENTS

Salad

2 large fennel bulbs

2 oranges, peeled

1 shallot, finely minced

4 tablespoons dried cranberries

3 tablespoons, sliced roasted almonds (See Oven Roasted Nuts, page 44)

2 tablespoon fresh mint, minced

Salt, to taste

Freshly ground black pepper, to taste

Vinaigrette Dressing

4 tablespoons extra-virgin olive oil

4 tablespoons red wine vinegar

1 Core the fennel bulbs by cutting a V in the base. Trim off the feathery leaves and "fingers," leaving just the bulbs. Slice the bulb thinly.

2 Place the sliced fennel in a salad bowl. Peel the oranges and cut off the bitter white pith. Working over the bowl, cut between the membranes with a paring knife to separate the orange segments, letting any juice drip right into the bowl with them.

3 Add the shallot and toss lightly. Drizzle with the extra-virgin olive oil and red wine vinegar and season with salt and pepper. Sprinkle the cranberries and almonds over the top, garnish with the mint and serve.

Minted Beet Salad GF

MOST LABOO

Here's a Persian beet salad that is flavored with a bit of garlic and lemon juice, along with plenty of fresh mint. The yogurt's tartness contrasts wonderfully with the sweetness of the beets. To avoid staining your hands and your kitchen with the beets, wrap the beets in aluminum foil and roast in the oven.

Prep Time: 20 minutes
Cook Time: 1 hour
Serves 6 to 8

INGREDIENTS

6 fresh beets

1 cup (250 g) Greek yogurt

½ cup (15 g) finely chopped fresh mint leaves

3 cloves garlic, smashed

1½ tablespoons freshly squeezed lemon juice

1 tablespoon Sesame Seed Paste (tahini— page 42)

Salt, to taste

Extra-virgin olive oil, for drizzling

Mint sprigs, for garnish

1 Preheat the oven to 400°F (200°C). Cut the greens from the beets. Remove and discard the leaves and most of the stems, but leave a bit of the stem attached to the beet. Wrap each beet in foil. Place the beets directly on the oven rack and roast for about 1 hour, or until tender when pierced with fork. Peel the beets while warm and cut them into wedges. Place them into a serving bowl.

2 Combine the yogurt, mint, garlic, lemon juice, and tahini in a small bowl. Season with salt to taste and mix thoroughly.

3 Serve the beets topped with the yogurt mixture, drizzle with extra-virgin olive oil, garnish with a few sprigs of mint and serve.

Crunchy Broccoli Salad V* GF

This lovely salad, with its sweet and lively agave dressing, might not seem like a Silk Road creation; as any tequila lover knows, agave is a product of the Americas. But look again at the ingredient list and you'll see onions, which botanists believe originated either in the Middle East or Central Asia, and raisins, which developed in the Mediterranean. It's a Silk Road-inspired salad after all. The crunchiness of the raw broccoli and nuts and with the sweetness of the raisins makes for a delicious combination. The nuts pack a protein punch, and the salad sneaks in a healthy serving of the broccoli your family members might otherwise avoid, especially the little ones. As a bonus, there's very little time-consuming prep. You can even dress the salad ahead of time because the broccoli won't get mushy; just be sure to add the cashews and sunflower seeds right before serving, so that they don't get soggy. Thanks to Hedva Kessler, a member of the Great Neck, New York CSA, for sharing this luscious salad.

* Substitute Tofu Mayonnaise (page 48) for a vegan salad.

Mushrooms with Cumin V GF

Prep Time: 15 minutes
Serves 8

INGREDIENTS

Salad

2 heads broccoli, trimmed and cut into florets

½ red onion, diced

⅓ cup (50 g) raisins

4 tablespoons shelled sunflower seeds

⅓ cup (50 g) roasted cashews, halved (see Oven Roasted Nuts, page 44)

Dressing

¾ cup (175 g) mayonnaise or Tofu Mayonnaise (page 48)

2 tablespoons agave nectar

3 tablespoons red wine vinegar

1 To make the dressing: combine the mayonnaise, agave nectar, and red wine vinegar in a bowl and whisk until all the ingredients are thoroughly incorporated.

2 Combine the broccoli, red onion, raisins, sunflower seeds, and roasted cashews in a medium-size bowl. Pour the dressing over the salad right before serving and toss lightly.

The brightness of the lime and the earthiness of cumin mingle and are absorbed into the meaty mushrooms. Season with a good sprinkling of red pepper to give your palate a kick. The red pepper, lime, and coriander leaves are the common denominators for both North African and Thai cooking; both cuisines stress the balance of flavors. It keeps in the fridge well for up to 5 days.

Prep Time: 10 minutes
Cook Time: 20 minutes
Serves 4

INGREDIENTS

4 tablespoons olive oil

4 cloves garlic, minced

1 lb (500 g) baby bella mushrooms, quartered

2 teaspoons ground cumin

¼ teaspoon ground red pepper

Salt, to taste

Freshly squeezed juice of 1 lime

3 tablespoons finely chopped fresh coriander leaves (cilantro)

1 Heat the oil in a skillet set over medium-high heat, add the garlic and sauté, stirring and shaking the pan for 1 minute. Make sure not to burn the garlic; if need be, turn down the heat or briefly remove the pan from the burner. Add the mushrooms and stir quickly and constantly for 5 minutes.

2 Add the cumin, ground red pepper, salt, and lime juice and cook over low heat, stirring occasionally, for about 10 minutes, or until the mushrooms have released their liquid and most of it has evaporated. Let cool.

3 Transfer to a bowl and garnish with coriander leaves. Serve cold.

Curried Spinach Salad with Apples & Grapes V GF

This is a flirty and fruity salad that is so unique and elegant that it's perfect for a special affair. It's my signature salad that I bring to my Aunt Bracha and Uncle Yves' house every year for their potluck Thanksgiving dinner. Baby spinach and mushrooms are paired with apples, clementines, and grapes. Lady's finger apples work really nicely here, but feel free to use any crunchy seasonal apple. The black grapes add their honeyed, floral flavor and ambrosial fragrance. The curried dressing adds a warming note with its pungent spices, and the roasted cashews are sure to seduce you into a second helping. Thank you Janine for allowing this recipe to be exported from Johannesburg to my family in Forest Hills.

Prep Time: 30 minutes
Serves 12

INGREDIENTS

Salad

4 clementines, peeled

1 lb (500 g) baby spinach, washed and patted dry

1 lb (500 g) white button mushrooms, sliced

2 cups (200 g) fresh bean sprouts

2 apples, peeled, cored, and thinly sliced

8 green onions (scallions), green parts only, finely sliced

1 cup (175 g) seedless black grapes, halved

1 avocado

1 cup (150 g) roasted cashews (see Oven Roasted Nuts, page 44), for garnish

Salt, to taste

Freshly ground black pepper, to taste

Curried Dressing

1 cup (250 ml) extra-virgin olive oil

⅔ cup (135 g) sugar

1½ tablespoons curry powder

2 teaspoons gluten-free or regular soy sauce

1. With a paring knife, cut the clementines in between their membranes to separate the segments.

2. Combine the clementines, spinach, mushrooms, bean sprouts, sliced apples, green onions, and grapes in a large bowl. Gently toss all of the ingredients together.

3. To make the dressing: in a jar with a lid, combine the olive oil, sugar, curry powder, and soy sauce. Close tightly and shake until all the ingredients are thoroughly combined. Set aside.

4. Right before serving, arrange the salad in a serving bowl or on a platter. Then cut the avocado: make a deep lengthwise cut all the way around the avocado. Remove the knife and then twist the two halves to separate them. One side will still be connected to the pit, which you can then cut out with the knife. Cut the avocado flesh away from the peel in bite-size chunks. Working fairly quickly so that the avocado does not turn brown from exposure to the air, arrange the avocado pieces on the salad and pour the dressing over it, making sure to coat the avocado. (The acid in the dressing will prevent browning.) Garnish with roasted cashews, season with salt and pepper, and serve immediately.

Roasted Cauliflower Salad V GF

ZAHRA MEKHLA

Cauliflower is an ancient *cruciferous* (mustard family) vegetable that originated in Asia Minor, and went through many transformations before it reappeared as a staple in Middle Eastern cuisine. Eventually it found its way to the States and became a popular fall vegetable. This Middle Eastern salad represents the travels of a vegetable from East to West, intertwining with various cultures along the way. In it, cauliflower is roasted with onions and then tossed in a dressing enlivened with tahini, *za'atar* (the classic Middle Eastern spice mixture) and *harissa* (chili paste). This very filling salad can even be enjoyed as a light main meal.

Prep Time: 25 minutes
Cook Time: 25 minutes
Serves 4 to 6

INGREDIENTS

Salad

1 head cauliflower, cut into florets

1 red onion, chopped

2 tablespoons olive oil

1 teaspoon sesame seeds

Salt, to taste

Freshly ground black pepper, to taste

Spicy Tahini-Harissa Dressing

½ cup (125 ml) Sesame Seed Paste (tahini—page 42)

4 tablespoons freshly squeezed lemon juice

4 tablespoons warm water

4 tablespoons chopped fresh parsley

3 cloves garlic, smashed

1 teaspoon ground cumin

1 teaspoon Za'atar Spice Mix (page 44, or available in Middle Eastern markets and specialty stores)

½ teaspoon North African Chili Paste (*harissa*—page 43, or available in Middle Eastern markets and specialty stores)

½ teaspoon salt

1 Preheat oven to 450°F (230°C). Scatter the cauliflower and onions in an ovenproof baking dish and toss with the olive oil. Sprinkle with the sesame seeds and season with salt and pepper. Roast in the oven for 25 minutes, or until browned and fork-tender.

2 In the meantime, in a bowl, combine the tahini, lemon juice, water, parsley, garlic, cumin, *za'atar*, chili paste, and salt. Set aside.

3 Toss the cauliflower mixture in the sauce, cover and refrigerate for at least 1 hour or up to 2 days before serving. Serve chilled or at room temperature.

Middle Eastern Lemon Potato Salad v GF

Americans love creamy potato salads with either sour cream or mayonnaise; this lemony version is far more healthful and has a tangy flavor. Boiled potatoes are cubed and tossed with lemon juice, red onions, and dill, which give it a bright and cheery disposition. This is a perfect picnic salad and it pairs nicely with a Persian Green Frittata (page 58). It will keep for up to a week in the fridge in a sealed container.

Prep Time: 20 minutes, plus several hours to cool
Cook Time: 20 minutes
Serves 4 to 6

INGREDIENTS

3 lbs (1.5 kg) potatoes (8 potatoes)
⅓ cup (80 ml) freshly squeezed lemon juice
4 tablespoons chopped fresh dill
1 teaspoon sugar
1½ teaspoons salt
¼ teaspoon freshly ground black pepper
⅔ cup (165 ml) olive oil
½ red onion, diced

1 Put the potatoes in a large saucepan and add water to cover. Bring to a boil; then reduce the heat and simmer, covered, for 20 minutes or until the potatoes are fork-tender. Drain. When cooled, peel the potatoes, cut them into large cubes and place them into a large bowl.

2 Combine the lemon juice, dill, sugar, salt, and pepper in a medium-size bowl. Whisk in the olive oil in a slow stream.

3 Drizzle the dressing over the warm potatoes and toss gently to coat. Add the diced onion, toss just to combine, and let stand at room temperature for 30 minutes, so that the potatoes can absorb the flavors of the other ingredients. Cover and refrigerate for several hours. Serve chilled or at room temperature.

"This is the perfect picnic salad."

Raw Beet Salad in Lime Vinaigrette

V GF

This sweet, earthy, and delightfully crunchy salad is a powerhouse of flavor and nutrients. The lime awakens your palate to the gentle undertone of the daikon radish, which carries you away to the Far East. And you can quickly prepare much of it in the food processor.

Prep Time: 15 minutes
Serves 4

INGREDIENTS

Salad

1 beet, trimmed and sliced into thin matchsticks

1 large carrot, sliced into thin matchsticks

1 daikon radish, sliced into thin matchsticks

4 green onions (scallions), green parts only, finely sliced

Salt, to taste

Freshly ground black pepper, to taste

4 tablespoons finely chopped fresh coriander leaves (cilantro)

Lime Vinaigrette

Freshly squeezed juice of 2 limes

4 tablespoons extra-virgin olive oil

2 teaspoons Dijon mustard

1 teaspoon agave nectar

1 Combine the beets, carrots, and daikon radish with the green onions in a medium-size bowl. Season with salt and pepper.
2 Whisk together the lime juice, oil, mustard, and agave nectar in a small bowl and pour over the salad. Toss and adjust the seasoning as necessary. Toss again with the coriander leaves and serve.

Carrot Salad with Garlic & Lemon

V GF

This dish is perfect if you want to clear out a glut of carrots in the fridge and make a sunny Mediterranean salad. The lemon juice adds brightness, while the olive oil, garlic, and chopped coriander leaves perfume the carrots. The key is to allow as much time as possible for the flavors to mellow and marry. This salad can be eaten warm or cold, and kept in the fridge for up to a week.

Prep Time: 10 minutes
Cook Time: 10 minutes
Serves 4

INGREDIENTS

4 tablespoons olive oil

4 cloves garlic, smashed

8 carrots, cut into ¼-in (6-mm) rounds

½ teaspoon salt

Freshly squeezed juice of 1 lemon

½ cup (15 g) finely chopped fresh coriander leaves (cilantro— divided use)

1 Heat the oil in a medium-size saucepan set over medium heat. Sauté the garlic lightly, stirring and shaking the pan frequently, for 30 seconds to 1 minute, until fragrant. Make sure the garlic does not brown.
2 Stir in the cut carrots and reduce the heat. Add the salt and lemon juice and simmer, covered, for 7 minutes, or until the carrots soften.
3 Reserve about 2 tablespoons of the coriander leaves for garnish. Stir in the rest. Serve hot or cold.

Red Cabbage Slaw with Tahini Dressing

V GF

Red cabbage is one of the most underutilized vegetables in salads, yet its vibrant blue-violet color is gorgeous and it's so rich in antioxidants that it's one of the most healthful vegetables around. This cool Mediterranean slaw in a sesame paste dressing makes a perfect antidote to those hot summer days.

Prep Time: 30 minutes,
 plus 15 minutes to marinade
Serves 6 to 8

INGREDIENTS

Salad

1 small head red cabbage, cored and sliced into thin threads

1 large carrot, cut into thin matchsticks

1 green bell pepper, seeded, pith removed, and cut into thin matchsticks

1 yellow bell pepper, seeded, pith removed, and cut into thin matchsticks

Tahini Dressing

¾ cup (180 ml) Sesame Seed Paste (page 42)

⅓ cup (85 ml) water

4 tablespoons chopped fresh parsley

3 tablespoons freshly squeezed lemon juice

1 clove garlic, smashed

1 teaspoon salt

⅛ teaspoon freshly ground black pepper

1 Combine the cabbage, carrots, and green and yellow bell peppers in a bowl.

2 Stir together the tahini, water, parsley, lemon juice, garlic, salt, and pepper in a small bowl, and whisk until combined well.

3 Toss the cabbage salad with the dressing and let stand for at least 15 minutes before serving so that the cabbage can absorb the other flavors.

Bukharian Tomato Salad V GF

SHAKARAP

Bukharian cuisine is influenced by local agriculture, so the only time to eat this salad is when you have locally grown, vine-ripened tomatoes. Anything short of that will just not do for this simply seasoned salad. The closest thing to this salad is the Italian bruschetta, which also relies on the freshest tomatoes for the most striking taste. *Shakarap* is a simple, yet absolutely irresistible combination of very thinly sliced red onions, tomatoes, ground black pepper, salt, a squeeze of lemon and a drizzle of olive oil. It is a traditional Bukharian/Uzbek salad that goes especially well with the rice entrees.

Prep Time: 15 minutes
Serves 4

INGREDIENTS

1 lb (500 g) firm, vine-ripened tomatoes, thinly sliced

1 red onion, thinly sliced

Freshly squeezed juice of 1 lemon

Extra-virgin olive oil, for drizzling

Salt, to taste

Freshly ground black pepper, to taste

1 Combine the tomatoes, onion, and lemon juice in a large bowl.

2 Drizzle with olive oil and season with salt and pepper. Serve immediately.

Quinoa Salad with Parsley & Tomatoes TABBOULEH V GF

Prep Time: 15 minutes, plus 30 minutes for marinating
Cook Time: 30 minutes
Serves 6

INGREDIENTS

1 cup (225 g) quinoa

1 cup (25 g) finely chopped fresh parsley

1 small red onion, diced

3 tomatoes, finely chopped

4 tablespoons finely chopped fresh mint

½ cup (125 ml) freshly squeezed lemon juice

½ cup (125 ml) extra-virgin olive oil

Salt, to taste

Freshly ground black pepper, to taste

6 leaves romaine lettuce

Lemon wedges, for garnish

Tabbouleh is a lovely starter salad, originating in the Middle East, traditionally made with bulgur wheat and lots of parsley, mint and lemon. I've come up with this gluten-free version, using quinoa, the super-grain from South America. It's refreshing, tangy, and easy to make, and it can take on many different personalities, depending on who is preparing it. You can adjust these ingredients to suit your palate; however, the main rule is to use a lot of parsley.

1 Cook the quinoa according to package instructions. Drain and set aside until cool.

2 Toss together the quinoa, parsley, onions, tomatoes, mint, lemon juice, and olive oil, and season to taste with salt and black pepper. Cover and refrigerate for at least 30 minutes.

3 Place a lettuce leaf on each of 6 plates. Put a scoop of tabbouleh on each. Serve garnished with lemon wedges.

Roasted Carrots with Feta & Parsley GF

This salad elevates the humble carrot into a Mediterranean delight. The carrots are roasted to a delicious intensity of flavor and sprinkled with feta cheese and parsley. This is the kind of salad that can be served on the side, but it's so flavorful that it can take center stage as a light lunch with a side of Mushroom Wild Rice (page 145). Elegant, simple, and so tasty!

Prep Time: 15 minutes
Cook Time: 25 minutes
Serves 4

INGREDIENTS

- 3 lbs (1.5 kg) carrots (about 10), sliced on the bias about 1 in (2.5 cm) thick
- 3 tablespoons olive oil
- Salt, to taste
- Freshly ground black pepper, to taste
- ⅓ cup (45 g) crumbled regular or reduced-fat feta cheese
- 2 tablespoons chopped fresh parsley

1 Preheat the oven to 425°F (220°C). Toss the carrots with the olive oil on a baking sheet and season with salt and pepper. Roast for 20 to 25 minutes, or until browned and tender.

2 Once cooled, transfer to a bowl and combine with the feta and parsley. Toss lightly and serve.

Israeli Chopped Salad v GF

SALAT YERAKOT

This most famous Israeli salad is served in pita pockets, and at Israeli breakfast buffets. It is a favorite among the *kibbutzim* (the folks who work on the farms). Almost every Jewish community that has immigrated to the country has created their own signature variation. For example, Jews from India prepare it with the addition of finely chopped ginger and green chili peppers, North African Jews add preserved lemon peel and cayenne pepper while the Persian salad known as *salad shiraz* includes mint. When my mother and her siblings migrated to Israel from Afghanistan, they went to a *kibbutz*, where this salad became my family's "house salad." I prepare this salad during the short summer window when tomatoes are sugary sweet. The key is to use very fresh vegetables and chop them as finely as possible. When I want this salad as a main meal, I may add cooked chickpeas or feta cheese.

Prep Time: 15 minutes
Serves 6

INGREDIENTS

6 Persian cucumbers or 2 English cucumbers, diced

4 firm, ripe tomatoes, seeded and diced

½ red onion, cubed, or 4 green onions (scallions), finely sliced

½ cup (15 g) chopped fresh parsley

4 tablespoons fresh minced mint leaves

4 tablespoons extra-virgin olive oil

Freshly squeezed juice of 1 lemon

Salt, to taste

Freshly ground black pepper, to taste

1 Toss the cucumbers, tomatoes, onion, parsley, and mint together in a bowl.

2 Drizzle the olive oil and lemon juice over the salad and toss to coat. Season with salt and pepper and serve immediately.

Roasted Beet & Nectarine Salad v GF

This is what I call a sustainable salad. It makes use of the beets and their greens. The nectarines complement the beets sweetly and the lime dressing really brings out the flavors of this lovely salad. Roasting the beets in foil means you can skip all the mess that comes with boiling them, including the red stains on the pots.

Prep Time: 15 minutes, plus 1 hour for standing
Cook Time: 1 hour
Serves 4

INGREDIENTS

Salad

6 beets with greens attached

3 nectarines, peeled, pitted and cut in ¼-inch (6-mm) slices

1 small red onion, diced

Lime Dressing

4 tablespoons extra-virgin olive oil

2 cloves garlic, smashed

Freshly squeezed juice and zest of 1 lime

1 tablespoon sugar

Salt, to taste

Freshly ground black pepper, to taste

1 Preheat the oven to 400°F (200°C). Cut the greens from the beets. Remove and discard the stems. Chop the leaves coarsely and set them aside. Wrap each beet in foil. Place the beets directly on the oven rack and roast for about 1 hour, or until tender when pierced with fork. Let the beets cool. Peel them, and then cut each into 8 wedges. Place them in a medium-size bowl.

2 Meanwhile, boil a saucepan of water, add the greens and cook for about 2 minutes, or just until tender. Drain and cool. When the greens have reached room temperature, squeeze them to remove excess moisture. Add the greens to the bowl with beets, and add the nectarines and onion.

3 To make the dressing: whisk together the oil, garlic, lime zest and juice, and the sugar. Season with salt and pepper.

4 Pour the dressing over the beet salad and toss to coat. Let stand at room temperature for 1 hour before serving.

Chapter 5
Main Dishes

This enticing group of recipes from countries touched by the Silk Road will rescue you from the rut of weekday menu planning. Many of these substantial and inexpensive stews, curries, and legume dishes are convenient one-pot meals, others are perfect for large groups, and some are both at once. And while the dishes reflect the diversity of regional tastes, they have in common their reliance on local produce and a mélange of spices.

These dishes are a modern Silk Road *entrepot*, in which New World ingredients are fused with ancient recipes, expanding our palates and our hearts. The meals presented here are meant for sharing; breaking bread together creates a unity that is one of the greatest keys to human health and happiness.

One group of dishes in this chapter deserves special mention. Stuffed vegetables, or *dolmas*, as they are known, date back to the golden age of the Ottoman Empire, where there would be one answer to a bountiful harvest: stuff it. Indeed, *dolma* derives from the Turkish verb *dolmak*, which means to stuff.

Almost every country along the Silk Road has been influenced by the Ottoman Empire's contribution of *dolmas*, with each country creating a variation on this specialty. Accordingly, the stuffed vegetables presented in this chapter cross cultural boundaries and reflect the many different cuisines I have experienced.

Dolmas are a beautiful way to showcase vegetables. It's also an ideal way to present a complete meal, combining hollowed vegetables with rice, beans, herbs, spices, and dried fruits. Preparing *Dolmas* is a bit involved, so I suggest reserving these dishes for when there's a special feast at hand. Invite family or friends to lend a hand with the chopping, stirring, and stuffing.

Persian Eggplant Stew v GF

KHORESH BADEMJAN

Khoresh, which means stew in Farsi, is derived from the verb "to eat." This stew is one of the more popular types of *khoresh*—a combination of eggplant and tomatoes cooked in pungent spices. Although eggplant was native to India, it arrived into Persia by the fourth century, where it quickly became a favorite vegetable. Today, Persia is Iran, but *khoresh* with eggplant and tomatoes is still a favorite. My mother regularly makes this stew, even though she grew up in Afghanistan, which borders Iran. The Farsi and Afghan languages are similar but have different dialects, much like the food. In theory, many of the dishes of the two countries mimic each other, but they vary according to what grows indigenously. This is my mother's version of the classic stew, which is typically served over basmati rice.

"A Persian stew poured on Basmati rice for a complete meal."

Prep Time: 30 minutes, plus 30 minutes
  for standing
Cook Time: 1 hour
Serves 4

INGREDIENTS

1 large eggplant, peeled and cubed

1½ tablespoons salt

3 tablespoons olive oil

2 onions, chopped

4 cloves garlic, minced

4 ripe tomatoes, peeled and chopped

1 teaspoon ground turmeric

1 teaspoon ground cumin

½ teaspoon paprika

½ teaspoon ground cinnamon

½ teaspoon freshly ground black
  pepper

Simple Steamed Brown Rice (page
  133), or your favorite rice, for
  serving

1 Place the eggplant in a colander set over a large bowl and sprinkle 1 tablespoon of the salt on it; this will tame any bitterness. Let stand for half an hour; then drain and pat dry with paper towels.

2 In the meantime, heat the oil in a large saucepan set over medium-high heat. Sauté the onions, stirring and shaking the pan, for 7 to 8 minutes, or until translucent. Stir in the garlic and sauté, making sure it does not burn.

3 Stir in the eggplant with the remaining salt and cook for about 10 minutes, until the eggplant softens and sweats.

4 Add the tomatoes, turmeric, cumin, paprika, cinnamon, and pepper. Reduce the heat, and simmer, covered, for 30 minutes or until the eggplant is thoroughly cooked. Serve over basmati rice.

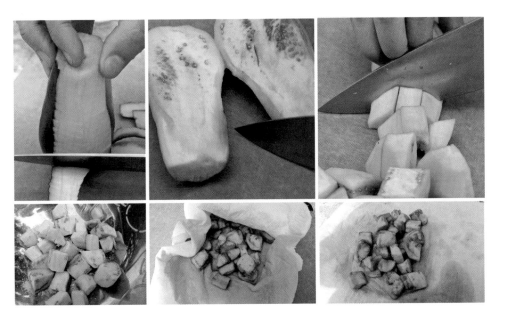

Sweet-Savory Chickpea Curry v GF

This South African curry is a result of the Indian migration to South African sugar plantations in the nineteenth century. This version is a twist on the classic; it has a sweet kick from fennel seeds, while raisins and carrots add a rich color and texture. My South African mother-in-law introduced this dish to me; the result is a fusion of flavors that is best served over basmati rice.

2 red apples, peeled, cored, and chopped

2 carrots, cut into ¼-in (6-mm) cubes

2 ripe tomatoes, peeled and chopped

½ cup (125 ml) Vegetable Broth (page 45)

1 tablespoon freshly squeezed lemon juice

⅓ cup (50 g) raisins

Simple Steamed Brown Rice (page 133), or your favorite rice, for serving

2 tablespoons finely chopped fresh parsley, for garnish

Prep Time: 15 minutes, plus 12 hours for soaking the beans
Cook Time: 1 hour, plus 45 minutes for cooking the beans
Serves 6

INGREDIENTS

¾ cup (150 g) dried chickpeas or one 15-oz (425-g) can chickpeas, rinsed and drained

4 tablespoons oil

2 onions, finely chopped

2 cloves garlic, minced

One 1-in (2.5-cm) piece fresh ginger, peeled and minced (about 1 tablespoon)

1 tablespoon curry powder

1 teaspoon salt

1 teaspoon ground cinnamon

1 teaspoon ground cumin

1 teaspoon fennel seeds

½ teaspoon ground turmeric

1 If you are using dried chickpeas, soak and skin them according to the instructions on page 29.

2 Heat the oil in a large saucepan set over medium-high heat. Sauté the onions, stirring and shaking the pan for about 7 minutes, or until translucent. Add the garlic and ginger and stir to make sure they don't stick. Cook for a few minutes, or until the garlic is fragrant.

3 Add the curry powder, salt, cinnamon, cumin, fennel seeds, and turmeric, and cook, stirring for 3 minutes to blend the spices.

4 Stir in the apples, carrots, and tomatoes and cook for a few minutes to combine the flavors.

5 Stir in the chickpeas and broth and bring the mixture to a boil.

6 Lower the heat and simmer, covered, for 20 minutes. Stir in the lemon juice and raisins and simmer for another 10 minutes.

7 Serve over basmati rice and garnish with parsley.

Afghan Squash Goulash v GF

BORANI KUDU

Kudu is Afghan for pumpkin, and it's traditional in this goulash, simmered gently with onions and ginger. The goulash is paired with yogurt, known in Afghan as *borani*. I grew up with this dish; my mother included meat to make it a more substantial meal. As a vegetarian, I think that with rice, this sweet and savory dish is filling enough. Pumpkin is a nutritional powerhouse; its color indicative of beta-carotene. Plus it's low in fat and calories. Its seeds are a good source of protein; roasted, they can be used as a garnish on the *borani*. If pumpkin is not in season, substitute butternut squash.

Prep Time: 25 minutes
Cook Time: 50 minutes
Serves 4 to 6

INGREDIENTS

Goulash

1 large onion

1 tomato, peeled

3 cloves garlic, peeled

One 1-in (2.5-cm) piece fresh ginger, peeled and minced (about 1 tablespoon)

4 tablespoons olive oil

1 small jalapeño pepper, halved, seeded, and diced

4 tablespoons sugar

1 tablespoon ground turmeric

1½ cups (375 ml) Vegetable Broth (page 45)

One 3-lb (1.5-kg) pumpkin or 2 small butternut squash, peeled, seeded, and cut into 3-in (7.5-cm) chunks

¾ teaspoon salt

Simple Steamed Brown Rice (page 133), or your favorite rice, for serving

Yogurt Sauce (Optional)

1 cup (250 g) plain yogurt

1 clove garlic, smashed

1 teaspoon salt

1 Purée the onion, tomato, garlic, and ginger in a food processor fitted with a metal blade. Heat the oil in a large saucepan set over medium heat. Sauté the onion mixture, stirring and shaking the pan for about 7 minutes, or until tender and golden brown. Add the jalapeño, sugar, turmeric, and 1 cup (250 ml) of the broth. Stir and bring to a boil.

2 Arrange the pumpkin or squash pieces in the tomato mixture, and season with salt. Cover and simmer over low heat for 30 to 40 minutes or until the squash is tender. Occasionally, move the pieces around gently with a wooden spoon so all the pieces cook evenly and the bottoms don't burn. Add ½ cup (125 ml) broth if the saucepan gets dry.

3 If you would like to make the yogurt sauce, in a small bowl, mix together the yogurt, garlic, and salt.

4 Serve in large, shallow bowls over basmati rice, with the yogurt sauce (if using) spooned over the top.

Simmered Red Lentils with Vegetables v GF

I never feel more present than when I'm preparing the vegetable mélange in this bright red dish. I feel the beauty of the moment as I infuse the red lentils with cumin, ginger, and the bite of chili powder and watch the whole thing simmer down into a creamy purée. Revel in this delectable entrée, which is best served over basmati rice. Thanks to my mother-in-law, Shirley, for sharing this recipe with me that is so aligned with my heritage.

Prep Time: 30 minutes
Cook Time: 1 hour, 25 minutes
Serves 8

INGREDIENTS

1 cup (200 g) dried red lentils, picked through for stones and debris

3 cups (750 ml) water

1 teaspoon ground turmeric

1 teaspoon salt

4 carrots, chopped into ½-in (1.25-cm) cubes

2 zucchinis, chopped into ½-in (1.25-cm) slices

1 cup (150 g) fresh or frozen green peas

1 small cauliflower, cut into small florets

2 tablespoons oil

1 tablespoon cumin seeds

1 onion, chopped

One 1-in (2.5-cm) piece fresh ginger, peeled and minced (about 1 tablespoon)

4 cloves garlic, minced

1 teaspoon chili powder

½ teaspoon dried red pepper flakes

3 tomatoes, peeled and chopped

Salt, to taste

Fresh coriander leaves (cilantro), for garnish

Simple Steamed Brown Rice (page 133), or your favorite rice, for serving

1 Wash the lentils in a bowl of cold water and keep changing the water until it runs clear. (This is very important so that the lentils don't get scummy.)

2 Fill a large saucepan with water and set it over medium-high heat. Add the lentils, turmeric and salt. Bring to a boil, reduce the heat and simmer, covered, for 20 minutes.

3 Stir in the carrots, zucchini, green peas, and cauliflower and simmer, covered, for another 20 minutes.

4 Heat the oil in a separate saucepan set over medium heat, and add the cumin seeds. Fry for about a minute, or just until the seeds pop.

5 Add the onion to the cumin seeds and cook, stirring often for about 7 minutes, or until golden. Add the ginger, garlic, chili powder, and red pepper flakes and stir for 2 minutes.

6 Add the tomatoes to the onion mixture, then reduce the heat and simmer, covered, for 15 minutes.

7 Pour the onion and tomato mixture into the lentil mixture in the saucepan and stir well. Then remove from the heat and let stand for 5 minutes in the saucepan. Salt to taste, garnish with cilantro and serve over basmati rice.

Red Lentil Curry v GF

DAL MAKHANI

Makhani is a hindi word for buttery. These lentils are richly flavored with spices, coconut milk, and tomatoes, and the whole thing is cooked slowly to achieve that buttery texture. The result is a delectably hearty curry. Lentils originated in Southwest Asia, but this dish is a staple of Northern India. The addition of lime lends an Asian flair that wakes up all the other flavors. The nutritious red lentils are sweet compared to their green and brown cousins, and are most suitable for stews. One of the advantages of cooking with lentils is that they don't have to be soaked first, like other legumes; this makes for a quick and easy dish.

Prep Time: 20 minutes
Cook Time: 1 hour, 15 minutes
Serves 6

INGREDIENTS

1 cup (200 g) dried red lentils, picked through for stones and debris

2 tablespoons oil

1 large onion, finely chopped

3 cloves garlic, minced

2 carrots, diced

One 1-in (2.5-cm) piece fresh ginger, peeled and minced (about 1 tablespoon)

2 teaspoons cumin seeds

2 teaspoons mustard seeds

2 teaspoons ground turmeric

1 teaspoon curry powder

1 teaspoon chili powder

1⅔ cups (415 ml) water

1⅔ cups (415 ml) Coconut Milk (page 49)

5 tomatoes, peeled and chopped, or one 26-oz (735-g) can of crushed tomatoes

1 teaspoon salt

Freshly squeezed juice of 2 limes

4 tablespoons chopped fresh coriander leaves (cilantro)

1. Wash the lentils in a bowl of cold water and keep changing the water until it runs clear. (This is very important so that the lentils don't get scummy.)

2. Heat the oil in a large saucepan set over medium-high heat and sauté the onion, stirring and shaking the pan for 5 minutes, or until the onions soften. Add the garlic, carrots, ginger, cumin, and mustard seeds. Cook for 5 minutes, or until the carrots soften.

3. Stir in the turmeric, curry powder, and chili powder, and cook for an additional minute, making sure not to burn the spices. (Adjust the heat if necessary.)

4. Add the lentils, water, coconut milk, and tomatoes. Bring to a boil; then reduce the heat and simmer, covered, for 45 minutes.

5. Stir in the salt, lime juice, and 3 tablespoons of the cilantro. Cook for an additional 15 minutes. Serve hot, garnished with remaining cilantro.

Indian Spinach Curry v GF

PALAK PANEER

One of the classic dishes in North Indian cuisine, this dish is typically made with *ghee* (Indian clarified butter) and *paneer* cheese. I've developed a vegan version, leaving out the *ghee* altogether and using tofu for the *paneer*, which is hardly noticeable because the tofu absorbs the wonderful flavor of the spinach curry. This variation is by far healthier than the restaurant versions that are swimming in oil. Serve over basmati rice flavored with cardamom pods for an authentic Indian experience at home.

Prep Time: 25 minutes, plus 30 minutes for pressing the tofu
Cook Time: 35 minutes
Serves 6

INGREDIENTS

Oil spray

One 16-oz (450-g) block of firm tofu, pressed and drained (page 27) and cut into ½-in (1.25-cm) cubes

2 tablespoons oil

1 onion, chopped

1 teaspoon ground coriander

½ teaspoon cumin seeds

½ teaspoon ground turmeric

1 teaspoon finely chopped fresh ginger

½ teaspoon chili powder

1 dried red chili

2 tomatoes, peeled and puréed

1 teaspoon salt

4 cups (240 g) trimmed and finely chopped fresh spinach, or one 10-oz (330-g) package frozen chopped spinach

Simple Steamed Brown Rice (page 133), or your favorite rice, for serving

1 Spray a large nonstick skillet with oil spray and set it over high heat. Arrange the tofu in a single layer and brown for about 4 minutes per side or until fully browned.

2 Heat the oil in a medium-size saucepan set over medium-high heat, and sauté the onion, stirring and shaking the pan, for about 7 minutes, or until translucent.

3 Add the coriander, cumin, and turmeric, and stir for a few minutes until fragrant. Stir in the ginger, chili powder, and dried red chili and cook for 4 minutes.

4 Pour in the tomato purée and stir to combine. Bring to a boil and mix in the spinach.

5 Add the salt; taste and adjust if necessary. Stir in the spinach. Cover and let simmer over medium heat for about 7 minutes, or until the spinach has turned deep green in color.

6 Gently stir in the tofu and combine well with the spinach. Simmer covered for another 5 minutes in order for the tofu to absorb the flavors of the curry. Serve over cardamom-flavored basmati rice.

Mushroom Curry V GF

This dish is an amalgamation of dishes from many different countries along the Silk Road. It features the apple, raisin, and nut topping characteristic of Persian and Bukharian cuisine. The creamy base for the curry is made with chilies and ginger, typical of Indian cuisine, while the coconut milk, which is often found in tropical Asian cuisines, tones down the heat. The liquid curry is so tangy and rich that it is the perfect complement to a rice dish, which will soak up all the flavors.

Prep Time: 30 minutes
Cook Time: 30 minutes
Serves 4

INGREDIENTS

4 tablespoons oil (divided use)

½ cup (25 g) blanched slivered almonds

4 tablespoons raisins

1 green apple, peeled, cored and chopped

2 small onions, thinly sliced

2 cloves garlic, minced

One 1-in (2.5-cm) piece fresh ginger, peeled and grated (about 1 tablespoon)

1 small jalapeño pepper, halved, seeded, and diced

1 teaspoon coriander seeds

1 bay leaf

1 lb (500 g) baby bella mushrooms, sliced

2 stalks celery, chopped

1 large tomato, peeled and chopped

2 teaspoons salt

2 teaspoons curry powder

½ teaspoon freshly ground black pepper

½ teaspoon ground cumin

½ teaspoon ground cinnamon

½ teaspoon grated nutmeg

¼ teaspoon ground cardamom

⅛ teaspoon ground cloves

½ cup (125 ml) Coconut Milk (page 49)

4 tablespoons chopped fresh coriander leaves (cilantro), for garnish

Simple Steamed Brown Rice (page 133), or your favorite rice, for serving

1 Heat 2 tablespoons of the oil in a deep skillet over medium heat, until very hot. Add the almonds, raisins, and apples, and cook until the almonds brown a bit and the raisins plump. Remove to a bowl with a slotted spoon and set aside.

2 Heat the remaining oil in the same skillet until very hot. Sauté the onions, stirring and shaking the pan for about 7 minutes, or until translucent. Add the garlic, ginger, jalapeño pepper, coriander seeds, and bay leaf and stir for 1 minute.

3 Stir in the mushrooms and celery, and cook for 5 minutes. Add the tomato, salt, curry powder, black pepper, cumin, cinnamon, nutmeg, cardamom, and cloves to the skillet. Simmer, covered, over very low heat for 10 minutes.

4 Just before serving, discard the bay leaf and gradually add the coconut milk to the skillet over very low heat, stirring constantly.

5 Transfer to a serving dish and garnish with the almond-apple mixture and fresh coriander leaves. Serve hot with rice.

Curried Lentil Burgers <small>GF DF</small>

These burgers were inspired by India's lentil fritters and our hamburgers. They're a perfect blending of both cultures' food-ways and together they form a low-fat, healthful, gently spiced, intoxicatingly aromatic burger. Rice and lentils combine to make a complete protein; in this burger they are slathered with Raita and Mango Chutney, which adds a spicy sweetness. The recipe yields a lot of burgers but leftovers can be frozen for later use.

Prep Time: 20 minutes, plus 4 hours for soaking the rice
Cook Time: 1 hour
Yields 15 patties

INGREDIENTS

1 cup (225 g) short-grain brown rice

1 cup (225 g) dried brown or green lentils, rinsed, and picked through for stones and debris, or one 15-oz (425-g) can cooked lentils

1 onion

3 cloves garlic, peeled

One 1-in (2.5-cm) piece fresh ginger, peeled and cut into large, rough chunks

4 tablespoons fresh coriander leaves (cilantro), finely chopped

3 eggs, lightly beaten

2 teaspoons curry powder

1 teaspoon ground turmeric

1 teaspoon salt

½ teaspoon red pepper flakes

Grapeseed oil, for frying

Lettuce leaves, for serving

Raita (page 43), for serving

Mango Chutney (page 48), for serving

1 Rinse, soak and cook the rice according to the instructions on page 32.

2 Pour the lentils into a saucepan and cover with a generous amount of water. Bring to a boil, reduce the heat and simmer for 25 minutes, or until tender, replenishing the water if necessary. Drain.

3 Pulse the onion, garlic, and ginger in a food processor until mostly puréed. Transfer to a large mixing bowl.

4 Add the lentils, rice, cilantro, eggs, curry powder, turmeric, salt, and red pepper flakes to the bowl. Mix until well blended.

5 Pour at least ¼ in (6 mm) of oil into a large skillet and set it over medium-high heat. Scoop a heaping tablespoon of the patty mixture, and carefully place the patties into the skillet in a single layer. Flatten the top of the patties. Cover and cook for 6 minutes per side, or until browned. You will need to work in batches. Be sure to replenish the oil in the skillet as needed. Transfer the cooked burgers to a dinner plate lined with paper towels and let stand for a few minutes to absorb any excess oil.

6 Serve on a bed of lettuce with *raita* and/or mango chutney.

Chickpea Dal in Coconut Broth v GF

Dal is an Indian preparation of *pulses*, such as chickpeas, that have their outer hulls removed. The standard *dal* begins with boiling the pulse in water spiced with some turmeric and salt and then adding various spices sautéed in oil, together called a *tadka*. The spices that comprise the *tadka* in this recipe are the most common combinations, although they do vary by region. The addition of coconut milk is widespread in South Indian cooking, and it adds a subtly sweet, nutty taste and creamy consistency that is just heavenly. Serve this hot with basmati rice on the side.

Prep Time: 15 minutes, plus 12 hours
for soaking the beans
Cook Time: 40 minutes, plus 45 minutes
for cooking the beans
Serves 6

INGREDIENTS

¾ cup (150 g) dried chickpeas or one 15-oz (425-g) can chickpeas, rinsed and drained

2 tablespoons coconut oil

2 onions, finely chopped

3 cloves garlic, minced

1 teaspoon mustard seeds

1 teaspoon cumin seeds

1 teaspoon ground cardamom

1 teaspoon ground coriander

1 teaspoon ground cinnamon

1 teaspoon ground cumin

1 teaspoon paprika

1 teaspoon ground turmeric

½ teaspoon chili powder

½ teaspoon grated nutmeg

1 thread of saffron

3 to 4 ripe tomatoes, peeled and chopped

½ cup (125 ml) Coconut Milk (page 49)

1½ teaspoons salt

Simple Steamed Brown Rice (page 133), or your favorite rice, for serving

1　If you are using dried chickpeas, soak, skin, and cook them according to the instructions on page 29.

2　Heat the oil in a large saucepan set over medium heat and sauté the onions, stirring and shaking the pan for a few minutes. Once the onions get a bit translucent, stir and add the garlic. Sauté for 3 to 4 minutes, or until the garlic becomes fragrant.

3　Add the ground mustard seeds, cumin seeds, cardamom, coriander, cinnamon, cumin, paprika, turmeric, chili powder, nutmeg, and saffron. Reduce the heat and cook for about 10 minutes, or until the mixture becomes fragrant. This is called the *tadka*, which will season the *dal*.

4　Stir in the chopped tomatoes and coconut milk. Season with salt.

5　Add the chickpeas and simmer, covered, for another 15 minutes, or until thick and creamy. Serve hot with basmati rice.

Persian Yellow Split Pea Stew v GF

KHORESH GHEMEH

This traditional Persian stew—a delicious blend of split peas, tomatoes and spices—is the star in the repertoire of every Iranian cook. I was lucky enough to learn this recipe from my Aunt Yafa who was married to a Mashadi Jew. I always looked forward to having an Iranian meal at my aunt's table, because it was a variation on my mother's Afghan cuisine. Not only is this dish rich with flavor; it is also a very easy one to make due to the simplicity of the ingredients. It's typically made with lamb; this is my vegetarian version. Traditionalists top the dish with a generous helping of French fries, but for a low-fat version, use sliced roasted potatoes instead. Serve in a tureen and ladle over basmati rice.

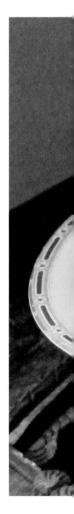

Prep Time: 25 minutes, plus
  3 hours for soaking the lentils
Cook Time: 1 hour, 20 minutes
Serves 6

INGREDIENTS

1 cup (225 g) yellow split peas

2 tablespoons olive oil

1 large onion, finely
  chopped

3 cloves garlic, minced

1 teaspoon salt

1 teaspoon ground turmeric

1 teaspoon paprika

½ teaspoon ground
  cinnamon

6 ripe tomatoes, peeled
  and chopped, or one
  28-oz (800-g) can crushed
  tomatoes

1 tablespoon sugar

2 dried limes (available in
  Middle Eastern groceries)

Freshly ground black
  pepper, to taste

Simple Steamed Brown Rice
  (page 133), or your favorite
  rice, for serving

1 Soak the split peas in warm water for 2 to 3 hours; then drain.

2 Heat the oil in a large saucepan set over medium-high heat; add the onions and garlic and cook, stirring and shaking the pan for about 7 minutes, or until light golden in color.

3 Add the salt, turmeric, paprika, and cinnamon, and cook for another minute. Add the tomatoes and sugar and bring to a simmer.

4 Break the dried limes into small pieces and discard the seeds as best you can. Add the dried limes and yellow split peas to the tomato mixture and simmer, covered, for about 1 hour. Monitor liquid levels, making sure that the sauce does not dry out. If you notice the sauce thickening too much, add 4 tablespoons of hot water. Once done, season with freshly ground black pepper and ladle over basmati rice.

"Traditionalists top the dish with a generous helping of French fries."

Stuffed Acorn Squash with Cinnamon-Spiced Apples & Raisins v GF

Consider this dish a study in autumn's bounty: acorn squash that has been brushed with sweet brown sugar and stuffed with chickpeas, apples, slivered almonds, and cinnamon. You can experiment with the stuffing and add different vegetables that you find in the farmer's market, like kale or Swiss chard, but be sure to keep the delicate spiced sweetness intact for that warm fall feeling.

Prep Time: 30 minutes, plus 12 hours for soaking the beans and 4 hours for soaking the rice
Cook Time: 2 hours, plus 50 minutes for cooking the rice and 45 minutes for cooking the chickpeas
Serves 8

INGREDIENTS

¾ cup (150 g) dried chickpeas, or one 15-oz (425-g) can chickpeas, rinsed and drained

1 cup (225 g) short-grain brown rice

3 cups (750 ml) Vegetable Broth (page 45)

3 tablespoons olive oil (divided use)

4 acorn squashes, halved and seeded

1 tablespoon vegan butter (available in most supermarkets)

4 tablespoons brown sugar

1 onion, finely chopped

4 cloves garlic, minced

2 carrots, cut into ¼-in (6-mm) cubes

1 Granny Smith apple, cored, peeled, and chopped

½ cup (75 g) raisins

1 teaspoon ground cumin

1 teaspoon ground cinnamon

1 teaspoon ground ginger

Salt, to taste

Freshly ground black pepper, to taste

½ cup (35 g) slivered almonds

1 If you are using dried chickpeas, soak, skin and cook them according to the directions on page 29.

2 Wash and soak the rice according to the instructions on page 32. Cook it with the broth and 1½ tablespoons of the oil.

3 Preheat the oven to 350°F (175°C). Arrange the squash halves cut-side down in a large baking dish. Pour in ½ in (1.25 cm) of water. Bake, covered, for 45 minutes, or until tender.

4 Melt the butter in a small saucepan over medium heat. Stir in the sugar, making sure the mixture does not burn. Remove from the heat. Turn the squash so the cut side is facing upward, but leave it the baking dish. Brush the cut side with the butter mixture.

5 Heat the remaining 1½ tablespoons of olive oil in a skillet over medium-high heat and sauté the onion and garlic, stirring and shaking the pan for 7 minutes, or until translucent. Add the carrots and cook for 5 minutes. Mix in the cooked chickpeas, apples, and raisins. Season with cumin, cinnamon, ginger, salt, and pepper. Continue to cook for 10 minutes, or until the vegetables are tender. Stir in the almonds and rice.

6 Stuff the squash with the rice mixture, and place the stuffed squash back into the baking dish and bake, covered, for 30 minutes. Serve hot.

Bengali Potato & Zucchini Curry v GF

Bengali cuisine is known for its mild flavor and multi-course meal structure. The zucchini and potatoes in this dish are marinated with salt and turmeric, which is typical in Bengali cuisine. (The spices act as an anti-bacterial and anti-septic in a hot, polluted region.) Although we in the West don't worry about unsanitary conditions as they do there, the spice mixture that I use is in keeping with the tradition of this dish. For a multi-course meal, start off with the Yellow Split Pea Dal (page 78), and then enjoy this dish over basmati rice, accompanied by *raita*.

Prep Time: 30 minutes, plus 10 minutes for standing
Cook Time: 50 minutes
Serves 4

INGREDIENTS

2 zucchini, trimmed and sliced into ¼-in (6-mm) rounds

2 large baking potatoes, peeled and cubed

½ teaspoon ground turmeric

½ teaspoon garlic salt

2 tablespoons oil

4 cloves garlic, minced

1 teaspoon minced fresh ginger

½ teaspoon ground ginger

3 teaspoons curry powder

1 teaspoon ground cumin

2 tomatoes, peeled and chopped

4 tablespoons water

1 teaspoon granulated sugar

1 teaspoon salt

Freshly ground black pepper, to taste

Simple Steamed Brown Rice (page 133), or your favorite rice, for serving

Raita (page 43), for serving

1 Combine the zucchini, potatoes, turmeric, and garlic salt in a large bowl and toss gently. Set aside for 10 minutes.

2 Heat the oil in a large skillet set over medium-high heat; sauté the zucchini and potato mixture, stirring and shaking the pan for about 7 minutes, or until slightly golden.

3 Remove the zucchini and potato mixture with a slotted spoon, allowing the oil to drain back into the pan. Set the mixture aside on a platter.

4 Return the same skillet to the stove and reduce the heat to medium. Sauté the garlic, ginger, ground ginger, curry powder, and cumin, stirring for 2 to 3 minutes, or until fragrant.

5 Add the tomatoes, water, sugar, and salt; increase the heat to medium-high and cook until boiling.

6 Add the zucchini and potato mixture, reduce the heat and simmer, covered, for 25 to 30 minutes, or until the potatoes are tender. Season with pepper to taste and serve over rice with *raita*.

Afghan Eggplant Moussaka with Garlic Yogurt Sauce BOURANEE BAUNJAN v* GF

Known in the Mediterranean as *moussaka*, this dish of layered eggplant and tomatoes with minced meat is similar to the Italian eggplant Parmigiana. The Afghan version is typically made with fried eggplant; however in this recipe it is grilled and then gently seasoned, layered with tomatoes, simmered in an oniony sauce and topped with green peppers. Simple ingredients create a powerful flavor, which gets even more oomph from the garlicky yogurt sauce.

Prep Time: 20 minutes, plus 30 minutes for eggplant standing
Cook Time: 1 hour, 10 minutes
Serves 6

INGREDIENTS

4 eggplants

Salt, to taste

⅓ cup (75 ml) olive oil (divided use)

2 onions, sliced into rings

2 green peppers, seeded and sliced into rings

4 ripe tomatoes, peeled and sliced

½ teaspoon ground turmeric

½ teaspoon ground coriander

¼ teaspoon ground red pepper

4 tablespoons water

Garlic Yogurt Sauce (Optional)

2 cups (500 g) yogurt

2 cloves garlic

4 tablespoons finely chopped fresh mint

Salt, to taste

Simple Steamed Brown Rice (page 133), or your favorite rice, for serving

1 Cut the stem ends from the eggplants and slice them into ¼-inch (6-mm) rounds. Spread them out on a tray and salt liberally. Let stand for 30 minutes, and then pat dry with paper towels.

2 Preheat the broiler. Brush both sides of the eggplant slices with the olive oil and season with salt. Arrange them on a large baking sheet and broil 6 in (15 cm) from the heat for about 5 minutes, or until browned. Turn and broil for about 5 minutes longer, until browned on the other side.

3 Heat 2 tablespoons of the olive oil in a large saucepan over medium-high heat and sauté the onions, stirring and shaking the pan for about 7 minutes, or until they are translucent. Transfer to another plate and set aside.

4 Place a layer of eggplant slices into the same saucepan. Top with some sautéed onion, green pepper rings, and tomato slices. Season lightly with turmeric, coriander, and ground red pepper.

5 Repeat using the remaining ingredients. Pour in the remaining olive oil and add the water. Cover and simmer gently over low heat for 45 minutes, or until the green peppers have softened.

6 If making the yogurt sauce, combine the yogurt, garlic, mint, and salt in a small bowl.

7 To serve, spread half the sauce into the base of a serving dish. Top with eggplant, lifting gently to keep the slices intact. Leave some of the juices in the saucepan. Top the eggplant with onions, green peppers, and tomatoes and the rest of the sauce, and drizzle the remaining juices over it. Serve with basmati rice.

* Garlic Yogurt Sauce is optional.

Afghan Cauliflower Curry V GF

GULPI CHALAW

Cauliflower originated in the Mediterranean, traveling from Portugal through the Indian Subcontinent and landing in eastern Afghanistan. It's easy to see the Indian culinary influence in this recipe, as it's most similar to the Indian *aloo gobi*. This Afghan curry is a delectable blend of sweet, spicy flavors while the cauliflower absorbs the tangy sauce. Serve with steamed basmati rice. A dollop of plain yogurt makes a heavenly addition.

Prep Time: 20 minutes
Cook Time: 1 hour
Serves 4

INGREDIENTS

2 onions, chopped

6 cloves garlic, peeled

One 1-in (2.5-cm) piece fresh ginger, peeled and chopped (about 1 tablespoon)

1 tomato, peeled and chopped

3 tablespoons olive oil

1 teaspoon ground curry

1 teaspoon ground coriander

1 teaspoon ground turmeric

1 teaspoon salt

½ teaspoon freshly ground black pepper

½ cup (125 ml) Vegetable Broth (page 45)

1 head cauliflower, washed, stem removed, cut into large pieces

Simple Steamed Brown Rice (page 133), or your favorite rice, for serving

Plain yogurt, for serving (optional)

1 Purée the onions in a food processor fitted with a metal blade. Transfer the onions to small bowl and process the garlic and ginger. Remove them to another small bowl and process the tomato.

2 Heat the olive oil in a large saucepan set over medium-high heat. Sauté the onions, stirring and shaking the pan for about 5 minutes, or until golden brown. Add the garlic and ginger mixture and cook for an additional 2 minutes. Add the curry, coriander, turmeric, salt, ground pepper, chopped tomato, and broth. Stir well and simmer for about 8 minutes, or until the liquid reduces in volume and you have a thick sauce.

3 Add the cauliflower and stir until the sauce covers all the pieces.

4 Cover and simmer on low heat, stirring every 5 minutes for 20 to 30 minutes, or until the cauliflower can be easily pierced by a fork. Remove the lid and cook for another 5 minutes to allow the sauce to reduce. The cooking time will vary, but you want the result to be fork-tender, not mushy.

Stuffed Peppers v GF

Stuffed peppers are a staple in almost every cuisine along the Silk Road. The moist rice filling reflects all those culinary cultures, combining allspice and tomatoes (from the Mediterranean) with the sweetness of raisins (prevalent in Central Asian cuisine). Put them all together and a wondrous fragrance will permeate your whole house. Choose peppers that can stand on their base. This dish presents beautifully as a main course with an Israeli Chopped Salad (page 98).

Prep Time: 30 minutes, plus 4 hours for soaking the rice
Cook Time: 1 hour, 35 minutes, plus 50 minutes for cooking the rice
Serves 6

INGREDIENTS

6 green bell peppers

Stuffing

1 cup (225 g) short-grain brown rice
2 cups (500 ml) Vegetable Broth (page 45)
1 tablespoon olive oil
1 onion, finely chopped
One 1-in (2.5-cm) piece fresh ginger, peeled and grated (about 1 tablespoon)
8 oz (250 g) button mushrooms, cleaned and chopped
½ cup (75 g) raisins, soaked in warm water until plump and then drained
1 teaspoon salt
½ teaspoon ground turmeric
½ teaspoon ground allspice
¼ teaspoon grated nutmeg
Freshly ground black pepper, to taste

Tomato Sauce

2 tablespoons olive oil
2 onions, finely chopped
4 cloves garlic, minced
2 tomatoes, peeled and chopped
1 tablespoon brown sugar
½ teaspoon ground cinnamon
½ teaspoon salt
Freshly ground black pepper, to taste

1 Wash and soak the rice according to the instructions on page 32. Then boil it, as described on page 133, substituting broth for the water.

2 Heat the oil in a skillet set over medium-high heat and sauté the onion and ginger, stirring and shaking the pan for 7 minutes, or until the onions become translucent. Add the chopped mushrooms and stir every few minutes to make sure they don't burn. Cook for about 5 minutes, or until the mushrooms have released their liquid.

3 Combine the rice, the onion mixture, raisins, salt, turmeric, allspice, nutmeg, and ground black pepper in a large bowl. Set aside.

4 For the tomato sauce, use the same skillet that you used for the onions. Heat the oil and sauté the onions and garlic, stirring and shaking the pan for about 7 minutes, or until the onions become translucent. Stir in the tomatoes, brown sugar, cinnamon, salt, and pepper. Bring to a boil; reduce the heat and simmer, covered, for 10 minutes.

5 Preheat the oven to 350°F (175°C). Cut the tops off the peppers, and remove the seeds and the pith.

6 Arrange the peppers in a large baking dish, and pack the insides with the rice filling. Spoon the tomato sauce around them. Cover with aluminum foil and bake for 1 hour, or until the peppers are dark green and very tender.

Turkish Baked Eggplant with Mint v GF

IMAM BAYALDI

This eggplant dish is one of the most famous dishes of Turkish cuisine, most likely because of the legends that surround its name. In fact, it's so famous that it has crossed borders into Iran, Bulgaria, Albania, and Greece. It is known everywhere by its Turkish name, *imam bayaldi*, meaning "the Imam fainted." Folktales vary as to why the Imam fainted. One theory is that he was appalled by the extravagant use of olive oil. Another tells of a newlywed Imam who fainted when he was informed that the olive oil dowry had been exhausted after just two weeks. The final legend is that Imam was overtaken with pleasure at the flavor when presented with this dish by his wife. I tend to favor the last one because this dish is delectable! Petite eggplants are stuffed with fresh tomatoes, onions, and garlic. These staple ingredients of the Mediterranean diet are so simple and yet so flavorful. The addition of mint to this dish adds an unexpected freshness.

Prep Time: 10 minutes, plus 30 minutes for eggplant to stand
Cook Time: 1 hour, 25 minutes
Serves 6

INGREDIENTS

6 Italian eggplants

2 tablespoons salt

Filling

1 cup (250 ml) olive oil (divided use)

2 large onions, thinly sliced

6 cloves garlic, crushed

¾ cup (20 g) chopped fresh mint

1½ teaspoons salt

1 teaspoon ground cumin

2 large tomatoes, peeled and chopped

4 tablespoons water

1 Prepare the eggplants as described on the opposite page.

2 To make the filling, heat 2 tablespoons of the oil in a large skillet over medium heat and add the onion and garlic. Sauté for 5 minutes, stirring and shaking the pan. Add the mint, salt, sugar, ground cumin, and tomatoes and sauté for 10 minutes or until tomatoes have softened. Transfer to a bowl and set aside.

3 In the same skillet, heat 4 tablespoons of the olive oil over medium heat. Carefully place the slit eggplants into the pan and roast for about 5 minutes, turning so that all sides are lightly browned.

4 Preheat the oven to 350°F (175°C). Place the eggplants in a single layer in a casserole dish facing slit side up.

5 Open up the slits in the eggplants with your hands and stuff each eggplant with the onion-tomato mixture. Drizzle the remaining oil and 4 tablespoons of water over them. Cover with aluminum foil and bake for 1 hour.

> "Ingredients of the Mediterranean diet are simple and yet so flavorful."

How to Open Up the Eggplant

1 Make a slit, lengthwise, in each eggplant without opening the ends, so that it forms a pocket.

2 Place the eggplant in a colander set over a large bowl and sprinkle 2 tablespoons of salt on it; this will remove the bitterness.

3 Let stand for half an hour, then drain and pat dry with paper towels.

Bukharian Stuffed Cabbage v GF

OSHI DOLMA

This *dolma* recipe comes from Bukhara, a city in Uzbekistan. The dish originated as a way to use up leftover food, particularly the rice dishes so prevalent in the region. Today, stuffed cabbage is a nostalgic dish reminiscent of the Old Country—indeed, it made its way west to Europe, and became a staple there, as well. Almost every immigrant family from the Silk Road has a version of *dolma* that's been passed down. The filling is based on rice, onions, and spices. The largest leaves can be used to wrap the moist, sweet fillings, while small pieces of cabbages are mixed into the tomato-based sauce. To cut down on some prep time, you can use a rice cooker for the rice, which I often do. Serve directly from the baking dish, garnishing with some lemon wedges and fresh parsley.

Prep Time: 45 minutes, plus 12 hours for soaking the beans and 4 hours for soaking the rice
Cook Time: 4 hours, plus 45 minutes for cooking the beans
Serves 20

INGREDIENTS
¾ cup (150 g) dried chickpeas or one 15-oz (425-g) can chickpeas, rinsed and drained
1 cabbage or 20 cabbage leaves

Filling
1½ cups (350 g) short-grain brown rice
3 cups (750 ml) Vegetable Broth (page 45)
3 tablespoons olive oil (divided use)
2 onions, finely chopped
4 carrots, diced
2 tomatoes, chopped
4 stalks celery, diced
10 oz (330 g) white mushrooms, chopped
2 apples, peeled, cored, and chopped
½ teaspoon salt
½ cup (15 g) chopped fresh parsley
½ cup (15 g) finely chopped fresh dill
2 teaspoons ground cumin
1 teaspoon crushed red pepper flakes
1 teaspoon ground turmeric

Tomato Sauce
4 tablespoons olive oil
2 onions, chopped
4 cloves garlic, minced
2 tomatoes, peeled and puréed
4 tablespoons Duck Sauce (page 47)
2 tablespoons Tomato Paste (page 42)
½ teaspoon ground cinnamon
½ teaspoon salt
Freshly ground black pepper, to taste
Lemon wedges, for garnish

1 If you are using dried chickpeas, soak, skin and cook them according to the directions on page 29.
2 Wash and soak the rice according to the instructions on page 32. Combine the rice, broth, and 1½ tablespoons olive oil in a medium saucepan. Cover and bring to a boil. Reduce the heat and simmer, covered, for 50 minutes. Remove from the

heat, and let stand in the covered pot for 10 minutes.

3 Place the whole cabbage, stem side down, in a large stockpot and add enough boiling water so that the cabbage is at least half submerged. Cook the cabbage, covered, turning it occasionally, for about 40 minutes, or until the leaves start to soften.

4 Heat the remaining oil in another medium saucepan over medium-high heat. Sauté the onions, stirring and shaking the pan for 7 minutes, or until they become translucent. Add the carrots and stir for about 6 to 7 minutes, or until softened. Stir in the tomatoes, celery, mushrooms, and apples. Season with salt and cook for about 7 minutes, or until all the vegetables have softened.

5 Combine the vegetables with the rice and toss with the chopped fresh parsley and dill. Add the cumin, red pepper, and turmeric and mix well to combine.

6 Remove the cabbage from the saucepan and let it cool. Gently and carefully, pull off the leaves one at a time. If there are cabbage leaves that are too small to fill, slice them and save them to line the bottom of the casserole dish.

7 For the tomato sauce, use the same saucepan as used for the vegetables. Heat the oil and sauté the onions and garlic, stirring and shaking the pan for 7 minutes, or until the onions become translucent. Stir in the tomatoes, duck sauce, tomato paste, cinnamon, salt, and pepper. Bring it to a boil, then reduce the heat and simmer, covered, for 10 minutes.

8 Preheat the oven to 350°F (175°C). Line a large baking dish with the surplus cabbage leaves that you could not use for the filling.

9 Place 2 heaping tablespoons of filling onto the edge of each cabbage leaf and roll it into a neat cigar shape (although larger), folding in the sides as you go.

10 Arrange the stuffed cabbages in the baking dish, seam-side down. Pour the tomato sauce over them and pour the cooked chickpeas on top of that. Cover and bake for 2 hours.

How to Fold the Stuffed Cabbage

1 Place a leaf on the cutting board, stem end closest to you.

2 Place 2 heaping tablespoons of filling at the base of the leaf, centered, about ½ in (1.25 cm) above the edge.

3 Fold the base of the leaf up and over the filling till it's completely covered.

4 Fold the edges of the leaf inward.

5 Continue rolling the leaf till it's completely rolled. This will create a neat package that has a better chance of holding together in the pot.

Bukharian Stuffed Onions v GF

OSH PIYOZI

This festive, special-occasion dish was typically made with ground meat that was delicately sweetened with dried fruits and then stuffed into the onions. My version is stuffed with a rice mixture that is seasoned in much the same way as the classic *osh piyozi*. Although there are a lot of ingredients here, most are readily available in your kitchen. This dish is perfect for gathering friends around and making a day of cooking together, because there are a number of steps. When I prepare it, I often invite my mother and aunts to help me and we make a fun day of cooking and laughing together. If you prepare this alone, try to set aside a portion of your day so you can meditate on each step and pour a part of yourself into this special meal. It will be well worth it.

Prep Time: 45 minutes, plus 12 hours for soaking the beans and 4 hours for soaking the rice
Cook Time: 3 hours, plus 45 minutes for cooking the beans
Serves 12 to 15

INGREDIENTS

6 large onions

Filling

I cup (225 g) short-grain brown rice

2 teaspoons salt

1 tablespoon olive oil

3 stalks celery, trimmed and finely diced

3 carrots, finely diced

1 apple, peeled, cored, and finely diced

¾ cup (20 g) finely chopped fresh parsley

5 dried apricots, finely chopped

5 pitted prunes, finely chopped

3 tablespoons Duck Sauce (page 47)

2 tablespoons Tomato Paste (page 42)

1 teaspoon ground turmeric

¾ teaspoon North African Chili Paste (*harissa*—page 43—optional for heat)

½ teaspoon curry powder

½ teaspoon freshly ground black pepper

Bottom of Saucepan

1 stalk celery, coarsely chopped

1 large carrot, coarsely chopped

Silk Road Tomato Sauce

2 large tomatoes, seeded, peeled and puréed

⅓ cup (75 g) Duck Sauce (page 47)

½ cup (115 ml) olive oil

2 tablespoons tamarind paste (available in Asian or Indian groceries or specialty stores—optional for tartness)

2 tablespoons Tomato Paste (page 42)

½ teaspoon salt

1 teaspoon ground turmeric

Topping

¾ cup (150 g) dried chickpeas or one 15-oz (425-g) can chickpeas, rinsed and drained

2 apples, peeled, cored, and chopped

5 pitted prunes

1. If you are using dried chickpeas, soak and skin them according to the directions on page 29.

2. Wash and soak the rice according to the instructions on page 32. Pour the rice into a medium-size saucepan and add 2 cups (500 ml) cold water. Season with ½ teaspoon of the salt and add the 1 tablespoon of oil. Bring to a boil over medium-high heat and continue boiling for 10 minutes. Remove from heat; drain in a colander and rinse with cold water.

3. Peel the onions and trim both ends. Make a lengthwise slit three-fourths of the way into the core of the onion. This will make it easy to detach the layers later, when it is cooked.

4. Place the onions in a large saucepan filled with cold water. Bring to a boil over medium-high heat, and continue boiling for 20 minutes, or until tender. Drain and let stand until they are cool enough to handle. The onions will be thick and will have turned white.

5. Combine the rice, celery, carrots, apple, parsley, apricots, prunes, duck sauce, tomato paste, 1½ teaspoons salt, turmeric, chili paste (if using), curry powder, and pepper in a large bowl.

6. Scatter the coarsely chopped celery and carrots into the same saucepan that you used for the onions.

7. Carefully separate the layers of the onions into individual shells. Place 1 tablespoon of filling into each shell and shape into torpedoes. Gently place the stuffed onions into the saucepan, one over the other on top of the celery and carrots.

8. For the sauce: combine and mix the pureed tomatoes, duck sauce, oil, tamarind paste (if using), tomato paste, salt and turmeric. Pour the sauce over the stuffed onions.

9. Scatter the chickpeas, apples, and prunes over the stuffed onions.

10. Cover the onions with an overturned plate that is slightly smaller than the saucepan. Bring to boil and then lower heat and simmer, covered, for 2 hours. Serve hot.

Persian Green-Herbed Stew v GF

GORMEH SABZI

This Persian green-herbed stew has been adapted from the Afghan *sabzi chalau*, which is more soupy than the Persian variation and is cooked with lemon juice rather than dried limes. When I was a child in my parents' home, this stew was served when my father returned home from his frequent international trading trips; it was the signature dish for the occasion of a family member returning home. It's nice to come home to a nourishing stew that immediately warms you up and envelops into your family. Both versions are made with the greens—spinach and parsley—which are cooked down into an olive-green, syrupy stew—and red kidney beans. The Afghan *chalau* is made with the addition of dill and lemons instead of dried limes, which infuses the stew with a restorative and refreshing tang—ideal for a jetlagged mind. Serve in a tureen with the dried limes for display, but do not eat them, as they are rather bitter. Ladle the stew over basmati rice.

Prep Time: 30 minutes, plus 12 hours for soaking the beans
Cook Time: 2 hours, plus 1 hour, 30 minutes for cooking the beans
Serves 8

INGREDIENTS

¾ cup (150 g) dried red kidney beans, or one 15-oz (425-g) can red kidney beans, rinsed and drained

2 tablespoons oil

1 large onion, chopped

2 teaspoons ground turmeric

2 teaspoons ground cumin

1 teaspoon curry powder

1 teaspoon ground coriander

1½ teaspoons salt

½ teaspoon freshly ground black pepper

2 cups (120 g) trimmed and finely chopped fresh spinach

2 cups (50 g) chopped fresh dill

2 cups (50 g) chopped fresh parsley

5 green onions (scallions), chopped

3 cups (750 ml) Vegetable Broth (page 45)

3 dried Persian limes (available in Middle Eastern Markets), or freshly squeezed juice of 1 lemon

Simple Steamed Brown Rice (page 133), or your favorite rice, for serving

1 If you are using dried kidney beans, soak and cook them according to the instructions on page 29.

2 Heat the oil in a large saucepan set over medium-high heat, and sauté the onion, stirring and shaking the pan for about 7 minutes, or until translucent.

3 Add the turmeric, cumin, curry powder, ground coriander, salt, and pepper. Stir for a few minutes, until fragrant.

4 Toss in the spinach, dill, parsley, and green onions. Stir until the vegetables start to wilt and become fragrant. Then stir in the broth and dried limes (if using).

5 Bring to boil and then lower heat and simmer, covered, for 1 hour, until the greens are a deep forest green shade and the stew has thickened. Add the kidney beans, and the juice of one lemon (if using) and cook for 30 more minutes. Serve over basmati rice.

Chapter 6
Rice Dishes

Rice is a fundamental food along the Silk Road, with each region preparing its own variation of a one-pot meal. Because it was the custom for large families to live together under one roof, it was necessary to create large meals from very little and for very little money.

Central Asia is unique in that there is no other region that has incorporated as many combinations of rice and embellishments into its cuisine. As rice spread westward, Central Asian cooks influenced North African and Middle Eastern communities to fashion their own versions. One theme among all these rice dishes is that they all feature interesting contrasts in color, flavor, and texture. Often these rice dishes will have a burnt bottom part, called *tadigh* in Farsi and *tardegih* in Bukharian. This is a sign that the rice was properly prepared. Eating the burnt part is a delicacy that is to be relished.

Although I grew up in a large family, even larger—much larger—was my extended family. Every Friday night we shared huge, lavish meals, all centered on rice. The rice entrees found in this section are amalgamations from assorted communities along the Silk Road, whose cooks have adapted the preparation of the grain to their local resources. I have further modified these rice dishes to create my own locally available, seasonal vegetarian repertoire.

Every rice dish here has a certain embellishment designed to give it a festive feel and satisfying combination of flavors. Some are colored with saffron or turmeric, or sprinkled with nuts and dried fruits.

A word to the cook: all of the dishes in this chapter are made with brown rice, which must be soaked before cooking. You should allow for two full hours of soaking the rice, unless the recipe specifies otherwise. The soak is part of the cooking process; it softens the rice, which allows the water to penetrate the grains. This prevents sticking and reduces cooking time. It also produces rice with a lovely, light texture, and releases enzymes that make it easier for us to absorb all the nutritional goodness in the rice. If you cook with white rice, soak it for 30 minutes and reduce cooking time in the recipe by 20 minutes.

Bukharian Mung Bean Rice with Garlic Oil OSHI MOSH V GF

This is a classic dish eaten among Bukharian Jews before a fast. It is made with mung beans, which are native to Asia and not widely known in the West. These are small round green beans that, when cooked, take on a porridge-like consistency. As with so many dishes eaten along the Silk Road, this one is influenced by other cultures. *Oshi mosh* is a variation on the Indian dish called *kitchari*, which is a staple comfort food in India. The word means "mixture" or "mess" as in "mess of pottage" or "mess of stew" or porridge. When you see it, you will know why, but I am here to tell you why you should try this jumbled mess—it is medicine. In Ayurveda—the ancient medical practice of India dating back 5,000 years—this mix of rice and mung beans is considered extremely easy to digest and is said to purify the digestion and cleanse the body of toxins. It is an ancient Ayurvedic practice in India to fast with a kitchari cleanse and, interestingly, this is the same dish the Bukharian Jews ate before a fast, as well. Kitchari fasting is actually a "mono-diet," which means the body receives a limited spectrum of ingredients and therefore needs to produce a limited number of digestive enzymes. The work of the digestive system is lessened, allowing for greater healing and cleansing to occur. *Oshi mosh* tastes like a cross between a creamy rice cereal and a light *dal* with the strong presence of garlic. This comforting, healing dish can restore sagging energy.

Prep Time: 10 minutes, plus 4 hours for soaking the rice
Cook Time: 1 hour
Serves 4

INGREDIENTS

1 cup (225 g) short-grain brown rice

1½ cups (300 g) mung beans, picked over for stones and debris

7 cups (1.75 liters) water

6 or 7 cloves garlic, smashed

⅓ cup (75 ml) olive oil

2 teaspoons salt

Plain yogurt, for serving (optional)

1 Wash and soak the rice according to the instructions on page 32.
2 Sort the beans, discarding significantly smaller and darker ones from the rest. Rinse thoroughly under cold water in a colander.
3 Bring 7 cups (1.75 liters) of water to a boil in a large saucepan set over high heat. Add the mung beans, and bring to a boil again. Reduce the heat to medium and cook for 20 minutes. If any skins float to the top, remove them with a skimmer.

> ## "A cross between a creamy rice cereal and a light dal with strong garlic."

4 Combine the crushed garlic with 1 tablespoon of water and 1 teaspoon of the salt in a small bowl and mash to create a paste.

5 Heat the oil in a small saucepan over medium-high heat and spoon in the garlic paste. Keep stirring to make sure the garlic does not burn; if need be, reduce the heat. Cook until the garlic puffs up. Remove the garlic and the oil from the heat and set aside.

6 Once the mung beans are cooked, increase the heat to high and add the rice. Bring to a boil and then simmer over low heat, covered, for 30 minutes. Stir occasionally to prevent sticking.

7 Season with 1 teaspoon of the salt. Spoon the garlic oil over the rice dish.

8 Serve with a large dollop of yogurt, if desired, to tone down the garlic. If you reheat this dish, add 4 tablespoons boiling water to remoisten it.

Swiss Chard Pilaf v GF

This dish has everything I love in a meal; brown rice with walnuts, which give it a hearty crunch, as well as raisins and ginger to tie the whole dish together with a touch of sweetness. The Swiss chard naturally soaks up all of the flavors while adding peaks of forest green to this robust dish. It is so filling that it can be eaten on its own or as a side dish.

Prep Time: 10 minutes, plus 2 hours for soaking the rice
Cook Time: 1 hour
Serves 4

INGREDIENTS

1 cup (225 g) long-grain brown rice, such as basmati

2 cups (500 ml) water

½ teaspoon salt

2 tablespoons olive oil

2 shallots, halved and sliced into crescents

One 1-in (2.5-cm) piece of fresh ginger, peeled and minced (about 1 tablespoon)

½ cup (75 g) raisins or currants

½ cup (60 g) walnuts, chopped

2 cups (120 g) Swiss chard, coarsely chopped

Salt, to taste

¼ teaspoon freshly ground black pepper

1 tablespoon finely chopped parsley, for garnish

1 Wash and soak the rice according to the instructions on page 32.

2 Combine the rice, water, and salt in a medium saucepan and bring it to a boil over high heat. Reduce the heat to a gentle simmer, cover tightly with a lid and cook for 45 minutes.

3 Remove the pan from the heat and set aside until ready for use.

4 Heat the oil in a skillet over medium-high heat. Add the shallots and sauté for 3–5 minutes, or until softened. Stir in the ginger and cook for another minute until fragrant.

5 Stir and combine the raisins and walnuts and cook for 3–5 minutes. The raisins will have softened and the walnuts will burn a bit. Stir in the Swiss chard and continue cooking for 4–6 minutes, or until wilted.

6 Stir the cooked rice into the mixture. Reduce heat to medium-low and cook covered for another ten minutes, stirring occasionally. Season with salt and pepper and garnish with the chopped parsley.

Simple Steamed Brown Rice

This recipe for steaming short-grain brown rice has just 4 ingredients; it couldn't be easier.

Prep Time: 5 minutes, plus 2 hours for soaking the rice
Cook Time: 30 minutes
Serves 4

INGREDIENTS

1 cup (225 g) long-grain brown rice, such as basmati

2 cups (500 ml) water

½ teaspoon salt

2 tablespoons oil

1 Wash and soak the rice per the instructions on page 32.

2 Combine the rice, water, salt, and oil in a medium saucepan and bring it to a boil over high heat. Reduce the heat to a gentle simmer, cover tightly with a lid and cook for 30 minutes. Note: if you lift the lid to peek or stir, the rice will not cook evenly.

3 Remove the pan from the heat and let the rice sit, covered, for 10 minutes before serving.

Boiled Rice KATEH

This is a simple way of making rice on the stove; however, the rice grains don't come out separately as they do in steamed *chelow* (page 136). The result can be loosely compared to sticky rice.

Prep Time: 5 minutes, plus 2 hours for soaking the rice
Cook Time: 45 minutes
Serves 8

INGREDIENTS

3 cups (675 g) long-grain brown rice, such as basmati

6 cups (1.5 liters) water

1 teaspoon salt

2 tablespoons oil

1 Wash and soak the rice per the instructions on page 32.

2 Transfer the drained rice to a large saucepan and add the water, salt, and oil. Bring to a boil.

3 Cover the pot and simmer for 45 minutes, or until the water is absorbed and the rice is tender. (Simmer for 15 minutes for white rice.) Remove from the heat and let stand, covered, for an additional 10 minutes before serving.

4 Fluff the rice with a fork and transfer it into a serving dish.

Bukharian Green-Herbed Rice v GF

BAKSH

This rice dish is a variation on the original, which included meat and was seasoned with various green herbs. It was typically eaten as the Sabbath evening meal along with several little starters. This version has more substance and can stand on its own—with added spices, mushrooms in place of the meat, leeks, parsley and spinach for the green color. Cilantro can be interchanged with the parsley if you prefer. Although it requires a bit of preparation, focus on the sacred act of combining and cooking vital ingredients. With your loving energy you'll create a wholesome meal for your household to enjoy throughout the week.

Prep Time: 30 minutes, plus 4 hours for soaking the rice
Cook Time: 2 hours 40 minutes
Serves 10

INGREDIENTS

3 cups (675 g) short-grain brown rice

2 cups (60 g) finely chopped fresh parsley

2 leeks

⅓ cup (75 g) oil (divided use)

3 large onions, diced

1 lb (500 g) white button mushrooms, sliced

3 stalks celery, diced

2 cups (120 g) trimmed and finely chopped fresh spinach

1 tablespoon salt

1 teaspoon ground turmeric

1 teaspoon ground cumin

½ teaspoon freshly ground black pepper

1 Wash and soak the rice according to the instructions on page 32.

2 Add the parsley to the rice and stir to combine. Set aside until you are ready to use it.

3 Prepare the leeks, to rid them of sand: Trim and discard the tough dark green outer leaves. Slice each leek lengthwise but leave the root intact. Hold it by the root to wash under cold running water. Separate the layers to get all the dirt out. When you are done, cut off and discard the root and slice the leeks.

4 Heat 2 tablespoons of the oil in a large saucepan set over medium-high heat. Sauté the onions, stirring for 7 minutes, or until translucent. Stir in the leeks and cook for 5 minutes, or until softened. Stir in the mushrooms and cook for 7 minutes, or until they begin to release their liquid.

5 Stir in the celery and cook for about 5 minutes, or until it softens a bit. Add the spinach, salt, turmeric, cumin, and pepper. Cook for 10 minutes, stirring occasionally. You will notice a lot of liquid in the saucepan; this will eventually steam the rice.

6 Add the rice to the saucepan with the remaining oil. Place a paper towel large enough to cover the pan on the surface. The ends will extend outside the pot. Cover tightly with a lid. Reduce the heat to low and simmer, covered, stirring occasionally for 1 hour and 30 minutes. (The towel will absorb the steam, preventing the rice from getting too sticky.) Taste to check whether the rice is fully cooked; if not, cook for another 30 minutes. A chewy black crust will form at the bottom of the pot.

7 When you are ready to serve, spoon the rice and vegetables onto a platter, and then arrange pieces of the crust on top. Serve hot.

Syrian Lentils & Rice v GF

MENGEDARRAH

This lentil and rice dish is native to Syria, although *mengedarrah* is a variation of the Bukharian *oshi mosh*. This popular dish spread across the Silk Road, gaining a different name in each region. Originally this dish was born of the Jewish holiday of Tisha B'Av, which commemorates catastrophes faced by the Jewish people. During the nine-day period before Tisha B'Av, observant Jews refrain from eating meat. Lentils are typically eaten on account of their round shape, which symbolizes a closed mouth and the cycle of life; it is the a food of mourning. Today, I eat this dish during the colder months when many vegetables are not in season yet, and I sustain my household mostly with legumes.

Prep Time: 10 minutes, plus 2 hours for soaking the rice
Cook Time: 1 hour
Serves 6

INGREDIENTS

1 cup (225 g) brown basmati rice

4 tablespoons olive oil

2 large onions, halved and sliced into crescents

4 cups (1 liter) water

1 cup (200 g) green or brown lentils, rinsed and picked through for stones and debris

1 teaspoon salt

½ teaspoon freshly ground black pepper

1 Wash and soak the rice according to the instructions on page 32.

2 Heat the oil in a medium-size saucepan set over medium-high heat. Add the onions and sauté, stirring for 10 to 15 minutes, or until golden brown. Pour in 2 cups of the water and bring to a boil. Add the lentils, and simmer, covered, over low heat for 20 minutes.

3 Add the remaining water, salt and pepper to the lentils and bring to a boil. Stir in the rice and return to a boil. Reduce the heat and simmer, covered, for about 20 minutes or until the rice is tender. Do not remove the cover during cooking.

4 Remove the pan from the heat and let stand, covered, for 5 minutes. Stir with a fork to fluff. Transfer into a large serving platter and serve hot.

Steamed Rice with Egg & Saffron Crust
CHELOW WITH TARDEGIH GF DF

This is the preferred preparation for rice along the Silk Road, and the method that I usually use. It involves soaking, parboiling, and then steaming the rice. The result is perfectly tender rice, with grains that are separate and not too sticky. The crispy crust that forms at the bottom is a delicacy with an omelet-like texture, and it's often grabbed off the platter before the rice. This is the most sought-after piece at the table. For extra flavoring and golden color, add bruised cardamom pods or saffron threads. *Chelow* is best made with basmati rice and is always served alongside a stew.

Prep Time: 10 minutes, plus 2 hours for soaking the rice
Cook Time: 1 hour
Serves 8

INGREDIENTS

3 cups (675 g) long-grain brown rice, such as basmati

3 tablespoons salt

Pinch of saffron, dissolved in 3 tablespoons warm water (optional)

1 large egg, lightly beaten

¼ teaspoon freshly ground black pepper

⅔ cup (160 ml) oil (divided use)

2 potatoes, peeled and sliced into ¼-in (6-mm) thick slices (optional)

6 cardamom pods (optional)

4 tablespoons water

"The egg and saffron crust is the best part of the dish."

1 Wash and soak the rice according to the instructions on page 32.

2 Bring 8 cups (1.75 liters) of water and the salt to a boil in a heavy saucepan. Add the rice, and cook for about 10 minutes, or until *al dente*. Pour the rice into a strainer and rinse with slightly warm water. (If you are using white rice, boil for 5 minutes.) Set aside.

3 If you are using saffron, let it steep in a small bowl of warm water until the color tints the water.

4 Combine the beaten egg, pepper, steeped saffron water, and 1 cup (250 g) of the *al dente* rice in another bowl. Mix to incorporate.

5 Heat ⅓ cup (80 ml) of the oil in a saucepan set over medium heat. If using the potatoes, layer them evenly at the bottom of the saucepan. Then spread the egg-rice mixture over the potatoes, or directly on the bottom of the saucepan if not using potatoes. Cook for 10 minutes over medium high heat. When it's hardened into a golden crust, mound the remaining rice on top.

6 If using cardamom, bruise the pods by placing each in turn on a sturdy, flat surface and rest the flat side of the blade of a large chef's knife on top. Push down on the metal surface with the heel of your hand and lightly crush the cardamom pod until the outer husk cracks. Do not crush too completely, or the seeds will fall out. Then, with the handle of a wooden spoon, poke 6 deep holes into the rice. Place the bruised cardamom pods deep into the holes.

7 Drizzle the remaining ⅓ cup (80 ml) of the oil and 4 tablespoons of the water over the rice. Then place 2 paper towels, one on top of the other, on the surface of the rice. The ends will extend outside the pot. Cover tightly with a lid. Reduce the heat to low and simmer. (The towel will absorb the steam, preventing the rice from getting too sticky.) Cook, covered, over low heat for about 30 minutes (15–20 minutes for white rice). If the rice is not fully cooked, add another 4 tablespoons of water and cook for another 10 minutes, making sure the rice does not overcook.

8 Scoop the rice from the pot with a wide spatula making sure not to disturb the crust that has formed on the bottom. Serve the rice on a flat serving platter, mounding it into the shape of a pyramid. Remove the *tardegih* from the bottom of the pot, in pieces, and place them around the rice, before serving.

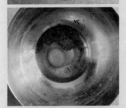

Preparing the Crust Mixture

See steps 3 and 4 in the method for details.

Fragrant Indian Pilaf

Along the Silk Road, every country has its own version of pilaf. Almost all pilafs feature a medley of vegetables made with basmati rice and seasoned with fragrant spices. The cardamom pods are used to impart their flavor, and never eaten whole, but can be used to ornament the dish. When my parents lived in India in the early part of their lives, they enjoyed this Indian variation of pilaf made with cloves, ginger, and saffron, and garnished with cashews and raisins. In my version, I have added green peas, green beans, carrots, and corn to add more color and substance to the assertive flavors in this one-pot meal. It's wonderful when served with *raita*.

Prep Time: 30 minutes, plus 2 hours for soaking the rice
Cook Time: 1 hour
Serves 6

INGREDIENTS

2 cups (225 g) brown basmati rice

4 tablespoons oil

4 cardamom pods

4 whole cloves

1½ teaspoons cumin seeds

½ teaspoon ground cinnamon

1 large onion, finely chopped

2 green chili peppers, seeded and finely diced

2 cloves garlic, smashed

One 1-in (2.5-cm) piece of fresh ginger, peeled and minced (about 1 tablespoon)

½ teaspoon saffron threads

2 carrots, finely diced

1 cup (200 g) fresh or frozen green peas

1 cup (150 g) green beans, trimmed

½ cup (85 g) corn kernels

4 cups (1 liter) water

1½ teaspoons salt

¼ teaspoon freshly ground black pepper

½ cup (75 g) roasted cashews (see Oven Roasted Nuts, page 44), for garnish

½ cup (75 g) raisins, for garnish

Raita (page 43) for serving (optional)

1 Wash and soak the rice according to the instructions on page 32.

2 Heat the oil in a large saucepan over medium heat. Add the cardamom, cloves, cumin seeds, and cinnamon and sauté, stirring for about 1 minute, or until the cloves begin to pop.

Spanakorizo GF

3 Add the onion, chilies, garlic, ginger, and saffron and sauté for about 5 minutes, or until the onions soften.

4 Stir in the carrots, peas, green beans, and corn and cook until the vegetables turn color, about 7 minutes.

5 Spoon the drained rice into the pan. Stir for about 3 minutes, or until opaque.

6 Add the water, salt, and pepper. Bring to a boil, cover and reduce the heat. Simmer for 35 minutes. Do not uncover during the cooking process. Remove from the heat and let stand for about 10 minutes before removing the cover. If any liquid remains, cook uncovered until it has evaporated. Fluff with a fork. Spoon onto a platter and garnish with cashews and raisins for a bit of crunch and sweetness. Serve with *raita*.

This Greek-inspired rice and spinach dish marries deliciously with walnuts and crumbled feta. Pair with a Bukharian Tomato Salad (page 95) for a light lunch, or Lemony Roasted Vegetables (page 162) for a light meal.

Prep Time: 15 minutes
Cook Time: 1 hour, 10 minutes, plus 10 minutes for roasting the nuts
Serves 4

INGREDIENTS

½ cup (115 g) brown basmati rice

½ cup (115 g) wild rice

3 cups (750 ml) water

4 tablespoons olive oil (divided use), plus more for drizzling

4 cups (240 g) fresh baby spinach, washed and patted dry

3 cloves garlic, smashed

1 onion, finely chopped

Salt, to taste

Freshly ground black pepper, to taste

4 tablespoons crumbled feta, for garnish

4 tablespoons roasted chopped walnuts (see Oven Roasted Nuts, page 44), for garnish

1 Wash and soak the brown rice according to the instructions on page 32.

2 Wash the wild rice by placing it in a strainer and holding it under cold running water for a minute. Swirl it around with your hand and then let drain. Pour the water into a large saucepan, add the basmati and wild rice and 2 tablespoons of the olive oil. Bring to a boil.

3 Cover the pot, reduce the heat and simmer for 45 to 55 minutes, or until the water is absorbed and the rice is tender.

4 Prepare a bowl of ice water and set it aside. Fill a large saucepan with water and bring to a boil over high heat. Immerse the spinach in the boiling water for 30 seconds; then remove it with a slotted spoon and drain. Plunge the leaves into ice water for about 30 seconds, to stop the cooking process. Drain again.

5 Heat the remaining oil in a large skillet set over medium-high heat. Sauté the garlic and onion, stirring and shaking the pan for about 10 minutes, or until translucent.

6 Add the rice and mix well. Fluff the rice with a fork, stir in the spinach, season with salt and pepper. Spoon the rice into serving bowls and top with the crumbled feta and walnuts. For a richer flavor, drizzle with olive oil.

Afghan Risotto V GF

SHOLA

Shola is a sticky, short-grain rice dish, cooked until soft in a tomato broth with carrots and turmeric, which together give it a warm pumpkin color. Typically, this Afghan dish is made with diced chicken; however, I have substituted chewy shiitake mushrooms, which only enhances the flavor of the rice dish. This is one of those enormous one-pot meals meant to feed large, multigenerational Afghan families; it's inexpensive, full of nutrition and packed with flavor to feed a household on the cheap. The soft-textured *shola* is typically served to babies just beginning solid food, to the elderly who have lost their teeth and to the sick for comfort. A refreshing undertone of lemon permeates this nutritious rice dish. This dish requires some nursing, with frequently stirring of the pot to prevent sticking. This act is a reflection of the care you take in soothing with food.

Prep Time: 30 minutes, plus 4 hours for soaking the rice
Cook Time: 1 hour, 30 minutes
Serves 8

INGREDIENTS

2 cups (450 g) short-grain brown rice

⅓ cup (75 ml), plus 2 tablespoons olive oil

3 onions, finely chopped

3 carrots, cut into ¼-in (6-mm) dice

3 stalks celery, cut into ¼-in (6-mm) dice

1 cup (100 g) chopped shiitake mushrooms

3 large ripe tomatoes, chopped

3 cups (750 ml) Vegetable Broth (page 45)

1½ teaspoons salt

1 teaspoon ground turmeric

1 teaspoon ground cumin

½ teaspoon freshly ground black pepper

Freshly squeezed juice of 2 lemons

1 cup (30 g) finely chopped fresh parsley, for garnish

2 green onions (scallions) green parts only, finely chopped, for garnish

> ## "This is an enormous one-pot meal meant to feed a large family."

1 Wash and soak the rice according to the instructions on page 32.

2 Heat 2 tablespoons of the oil in a large saucepan over medium heat, add the onion and sauté, stirring for 7 to 8 minutes, or until soft and translucent.

3 Add the carrots and celery and continue to cook, stirring often for 5 minutes, or until the carrots turn a bright orange.

4 Add the mushrooms, tomatoes, broth, salt, turmeric, cumin, and pepper and stir to combine. Bring to a boil.

5 Then mix in the rice and the remaining oil, and bring to a boil again. Reduce the heat and simmer, covered, for 55 minutes. Periodically open the cover and stir, making sure there is enough liquid in the pot so that the rice does not stick to the bottom. If the rice is too dry, reduce the heat and add 4 tablespoons water. This dish should have a risotto-like consistency that is soft and slightly sticky.

6 To serve, spoon the rice onto a large platter, sprinkle with lemon juice and garnish with parsley and green onions. To reheat, simmer in a saucepan over low heat and pour 4 tablespoons of boiling water on the rice to soften it.

Bukharian Pilaf with Kidney Beans & Carrots PILAU v GF

Pilau is the national rice dish of Bukhara and Afghanistan and is served at every large, festive gathering; indeed, it occupies center stage at almost every Sabbath meal. Being a vegetarian, I did not want to miss out on this traditional dish, so I updated it with kidney beans in place of meat. *Pilau* is generously seasoned only with salt and pepper, allowing the flavors of the carrots and onions to be the strongest element. The key to making *pilau* is to cook the ingredients in layers. The result, when you turn it out inverted, is a topping of meltingly soft, and in parts, caramelized carrots and onions. The rice is topped with cinnamon-infused raisins, which adds just a bit of sweetness to this peppery vegetable medley. On the side of the platter is a meltingly buttery garlic head to be shared and spread onto individual *pilau* portions. To cut down on time, you can process the carrots in a food processor, which will result in finely slivered carrots.

"Every Central Asian country has a variation claimed as their national dish."

Prep Time: 30 minutes, plus 12 hours for soaking the beans and 1 hour for soaking the rice
Cook Time: 2 hours, plus 1 hour 30 minutes for the beans
Serves 6

INGREDIENTS

1 cup (200 g) dried red kidney beans

2 cups (450 g) brown basmati rice

2½ teaspoons salt (divided use)

½ cup (75 g) raisins

⅔ cup (160 ml) oil (divided use)

3 large onions, finely chopped

½ teaspoon freshly ground black pepper

10 large carrots, cut into thin matchsticks

¼ teaspoon ground cardamom

6 cardamom pods

3 cups (750 ml) water

½ teaspoon ground cinnamon

1 head garlic

1   If you are using dried kidney beans, soak, and cook them according to the instructions on page 28.

2   In the meantime, following the instructions on page 32, wash the rice until the water runs clear. Drain and pour the rice into a large bowl with 1 teaspoon of the salt and pour boiling water over it. Mix well and let it soak for 1 hour. Drain and set aside.

3   Plump the raisins in a small bowl of warm water.

4   Heat 4 tablespoons of the oil in a large saucepan set over medium-high heat. Sauté the onions, stirring, for 7 minutes, or until softened. Then add the kidney beans, season with 1 teaspoon of the salt and ½ teaspoon pepper and cook for 5 minutes, stirring occasionally. Pat down the mixture with the bottom of your spoon to form a fairly even layer.

5   Make another layer with the carrots and season with remaining ½ teaspoon of salt and ground cardamom. Make sure not to combine the carrots with the onions.

6   Spoon the rice over the carrots. Distribute it evenly over the top.

7   Bruise the cardamom pods: Place the pods on a flat surface, place the flat blade of a large chef's knife on top of them and press down on it with the heel of your hand to crush them lightly until the outer husk cracks. Poke some holes into the rice and place the bruised cardamom pods into the holes. Pour 3 cups (750 ml) water and the remaining oil over the rice in a circular motion.

8   Drain the water from the raisins and season with cinnamon.

9   With a spoon, form a pocket in the rice around the side of the saucepan, and place the raisins into the pocket. Firmly push the whole head of garlic into the rice in the center of the saucepan.

10   Place a paper towel large enough to cover the pan on the surface of the rice. The ends will extend outside the pot. Cover tightly with a lid. Reduce the heat and simmer, covered, for 2 hours, or until the rice is fully cooked. (The towel will absorb the steam, preventing the rice from getting too sticky.) Check the rice periodically to make sure that the rice did not dry up. If the water has dried up during the cooking process and the rice is still not done, add ½ cup (125 ml) of water.

11   When the rice is done, use a skimmer to gently transfer each layer onto a serving dish. First, remove the garlic and set it to the side of the platter. Then, transfer the rice, then the carrots, and finally the beans. Scatter the raisins over the top for a sweet accent.

Bukharian Slow-Cooked Rice with Dried Fruit OSH SOVO v GF

This soft, fruity rice, with its lovely, aroma and flavor, is a modern adaptation of traditional Bukharian Sabbath rice that was served in my parents' home nearly every Saturday lunch. Since cooking is not permitted on the Sabbath, the rice was cooked in a linen bag (called a *khalti*) immersed in a soup stock and cooked slowly overnight. This method significantly enhances the flavor, as the vegetables and fruits melt into a thick brown sweet risotto. *Osh sovo* was always made with pieces of meat; however, I have created a meatless version, instead adding beans. Fusing European influence into this dish, I have used vegetables typically found in the Ashkenazi *cholent* (another dish cooked by Jews of Eastern European descent for the Sabbath) and I cook it in a slow cooker. Cooking it in this method will not only allow observance of the no-cook rule on the Sabbath, but it will form a dark crust at the bottom of the pot that can be enjoyed as a delicacy on its own. You can easily prepare this in the morning and come home to an intoxicatingly fragrant Central Asian rice dish at night. It's a perfect meal in the dead of winter to make you feel satiated.

Prep Time: 25 minutes, plus 12 hours for soaking the beans and 4 hours for soaking the rice
Cook Time: 12 hours
Serves 8 to 10

INGREDIENTS

1 cup (200 g) dried red kidney beans

2 cups (450 g) brown basmati rice

½ cup (115 ml) oil

1 large onion, coarsely chopped

3 carrots, cut into ¼-in (6-mm) cubes

3 large tomatoes, chopped

3 potatoes, peeled and quartered

2 apples, peeled, cored and quartered

1 sweet potato, peeled and quartered

5 pitted prunes, chopped

5 dried apricots, chopped

2 tablespoons raisins

1 teaspoon ground turmeric

1 teaspoon ground ginger

7 cups (1.75 liters) water

2 teaspoons salt

1 Soak the dried kidney beans according to the instructions on page 28.

2 Wash and soak the rice according to the instructions on page 32.

3 When you are ready to cook, add the beans, rice, oil, onion, carrots, tomatoes, potatoes, apples, sweet potato, prunes, apricots, raisins, turmeric, and ginger to the slow cooker and cover with the water.

4 Turn the slow cooker to the lowest setting. Cover and cook for at least 4 hours, and up to 12 hours. Periodically check the pot to make sure that the water has not dried up. If it has, add ½ cup (125 ml) at a time. Cooking time is very forgiving, the longer it cooks, the more the flavors meld. Season with salt at the end.

5 Spoon onto a large platter and top with the crust from the bottom of the pot, if you can. Serve hot.

Mushroom Wild Rice v GF

When a gentle autumn breeze makes the colorful leaves outside my window sway, I am inspired to bring nature indoors in the form of vibrant, woodsy wild rice. This "rice" is actually a grass and not a true rice at all, but that hardly matters to those who love its rich, nutty flavor. Crimini mushrooms add chewy texture and a heartiness to this dish that makes it a perfect side for a Thanksgiving meal, accompanied by Cinnamon-Spiced Butternut Rings (page 160).

Prep Time: 15 minutes
Cook Time: 50 minutes
Serves 6 to 8

INGREDIENTS
2 cups (450 g) wild rice
4 cups (1 liter) Vegetable Broth (page 45)
1 tablespoon olive oil
1 onion, finely chopped
5 oz (150 g) crimini mushrooms, sliced
Salt, to taste

1 Wash the wild rice by placing it in a strainer and holding it under cold running water for a minute. Swirl it around with your hand and then let drain. Pour the broth into a medium-size pot and add the wild rice. Cook according to the package instructions.

2 Heat the oil in a separate skillet over medium-high heat, add the onion, and cook, stirring often for about 7 minutes, or until translucent. Add the mushrooms and cook, stirring, for 5 to 7 minutes, or until they release their liquid and it evaporates. Season with salt to taste.

3 Once the wild rice is cooked, add the mushroom and onion mixture and toss to combine.

Persian Lentil Rice

ADAS POLOW v GF

This simple rice dish is transformed into a cheerful meal with layers of lentils topped with meltingly soft dried fruit laced with saffron. Although it calls for simple ingredients, it morphs into a colorful, aromatic, and truly cheerful creation. With all countries in the Silk Road influencing each other's culinary sensibilities, this lentil and rice dish is a variation of the Syrian *mengedarrah*. Using ingredients that are readily available in your pantry makes this dish accessible to Westerners who desire a celebratory vegan dish.

Prep Time: 15 minutes, plus 2 hours for soaking the rice
Cook Time: 1 hour, 25 minutes
Serves 4 to 6

INGREDIENTS

2 cups (450 g) brown basmati rice

6 cups (1.5 liters) water

1 cup (200 g) green or brown lentils, rinsed and picked through for stones and debris

½ cup (115 ml) oil (divided use)

1 teaspoon cumin seeds

One 4-in (10-cm) cinnamon stick

2 cardamom pods, bruised

2 onions, peeled and thinly sliced

2 tablespoons sugar

2½ teaspoons salt

½ teaspoon freshly ground black pepper

¾ cup (115 g) raisins

¾ cup (115 g) dried apricots, sliced

Pinch of saffron, dissolved in 3 tablespoons hot water

1   Wash and soak the rice according to the instructions on page 32.

2   Bring 3 cups (750 ml) water to a boil in a small saucepan and add the lentils. Return to a boil and then lower the heat to medium and cook for 15 minutes. Drain.

3   Heat 4 tablespoons of the oil in a large skillet with a deep rim over medium-high heat. Add the cumin, cinnamon, and cardamom, and cook until fragrant. Add the onions, sugar, and salt, and sauté, stirring for 15 minutes, or until golden brown. The sugar will help caramelize the onions, while the salt will accelerate the cooking process.

4   Add the lentils and pepper and mix gently to combine.

> "The simple ingredients morph into a colorful, aromatic, and cheerful creation."

5 Transfer half of the lentils to a bowl and set aside. Spread the remaining lentils in the skillet, and then layer in the rice and the remaining lentils from the bowl. Pour 3 cups (750 ml) of water over the top. Arrange the raisins on one half of the mixture and the apricots on the other. Bring to a boil, cover and simmer over medium heat for 20 minutes.

6 Drizzle the remaining oil and the saffron water over the rice. Cover and cook for 25 minutes longer. Remove from the heat and let stand for 10 minutes without uncovering. Transfer to a large serving platter and serve hot.

Bukharian Garlic & Chickpea Rice

SERKANIZ V GF

Serkaniz is a Bukharian *palov*, a one-pot main course meal typically made with rice, pieces of meat, cubed carrots, and garlic—lots of it—so garlic lovers; rejoice. Although there is a lot of fresh garlic, it adds more of a background flavor—you know it's there, but it doesn't have that strong garlic punch. Bukharian cuisine places a strong emphasis on garlic. For one, it's a natural antibiotic and Central Asians are big proponents of using the medicinal power of foods to heal. Uzbekistan (Bukhara) borders China—the largest propagator of garlic, which has influenced Bukharian cuisine. This *palov*—and there are many different versions—consists of sticky short-grain rice cooked with carrots, garlic, and chickpeas. Since it is customary for Bukharian families to live with a few generations under one roof, all the more necessary to make these large meals frugally. Bukharian cuisine is all about getting as much nutrition as possible into one pot to feed large families. This is one of the greatest Bukharian creations: a meal that has it all—vegetables, grains, and legumes wrapped into one exotic dish. Since short-grain rice can require baby-sitting at the stove, you can just as easily make this dish in your rice cooker.

"Garlic lovers; rejoice."

Prep Time: 25 minutes, plus 12 hours for soaking the beans and 4 hours for soaking the rice

Cook Time: 1 hour, 20 minutes, plus 45 minutes for cooking the beans

Serves 8

INGREDIENTS

¾ cup (150 g) dried chickpeas or one 15-oz (425-g) can chickpeas, rinsed and drained

3 cups (675 g) short-grain brown rice

½ cup (115 ml) olive oil (divided use)

2 onions, finely chopped

4 carrots, cut into ¼-in (6-mm) cubes

3 stalks celery, finely chopped

3 cups (750 ml) Vegetable Broth (page 45)

1 teaspoon ground turmeric

1 teaspoon ground cumin

1 teaspoon salt

½ teaspoon freshly ground black pepper

1 head garlic, smashed

Lettuce leaves, for serving

Tomatoes, cut into wedges, for serving

1 If you are using dried chickpeas, soak, cook, and skin them according to the instructions on page 29.

2 Wash and soak the rice according to the instructions on page 32.

3 Heat 2 tablespoons of the oil in a large saucepan over medium heat. Add the onion and sauté, stirring, for 7 to 8 minutes, or until soft and translucent.

4 Add the carrots and celery and stir until all vegetables are heated through. Pour the rice and broth into the pan and, if you are using fresh cooked chickpeas, add them now. Add the turmeric, cumin, salt, and pepper. Stir to combine. Cover and simmer over low heat for 45 minutes. In the last 15 minutes of cooking, if you are using canned chickpeas, rinse and drain them, pour them into the rice and stir to combine.

5 Check for doneness by tasting the rice and feeling if it is soft. If it is still *al dente*, place a paper towel large enough to cover the pan on the surface of the rice. The ends will extend outside the pot. Cover tightly with a lid and let steam for an additional 15 minutes. (The towel will absorb the steam, preventing the rice from getting too sticky.) If the rice is a bit dry, add 4 tablespoons water.

6 Pour the remaining oil into a skillet, add the garlic and sauté for a minute, or until the garlic puffs up and turns white, stirring often and watching the heat carefully to make sure that it does not burn. You are creating garlic oil, which is a prominent flavor in this dish. Remove from the heat. When the rice is done, pour the garlic and oil into the rice and mix well to incorporate.

7 Arrange the lettuce leaves on a large platter, spoon the rice and vegetables over them and arrange the tomatoes around the perimeter. Serve hot.

Persian Dill Rice v GF

SHEVID POLO

Behind the fenced courtyards in Central Asia, you may find dill hanging upside down to dry. I prefer to use dried dill in this *polo* as opposed to fresh dill, since fresh dill tends to clump in the pot and make the rice mushy. *Shevid polo* is the Persian equivalent to the Bukharian *baksh*, which is a green-herbed rice dish as well. This *polo* is simple; it calls only for a combination of rice slowly simmered with dill and lima beans to color the simple ingredients. Prepare the rice by soaking it in salted water and then parboiling it; this method is called *chelow* in Farsi. The *chelow* is then drained and put back into the pot to be steamed, resulting in an exceptionally fluffy rice, in which the grains are separated and not sticky. A golden potato crust is created at the bottom of the pot, to be layered on the rice as a crunchy and tasty embellishment.

Prep Time: 15 minutes, plus 2 hours for soaking the rice
Cook Time: 1 hour, 25 minutes, plus 2 hours 30 minutes for drying the dill and 30 minutes to rest the rice
Serves 8

INGREDIENTS

2 cups (450 g) brown basmati rice

1 cup (15 g) dried dill weed or 2 large bunches fresh dill

2 cups (150 g) fresh or frozen lima beans

⅓ cup (75 ml) oil (divided use)

1 teaspoon ground turmeric

1 teaspoon salt

2 potatoes, peeled and sliced lengthwise

1 Wash and soak the rice according to the instructions on page 32.

2 If you are using fresh dill, preheat the oven to 170°F (77°C). Wash the dill and trim the ends. Pat dry with a paper towel and then spread the dill on a baking sheet in a single layer. Bake in the preheated oven for 2 hours 30 minutes, or until the dill crumbles off the stem. Discard the stems.

3 To parboil the rice: Fill a medium-size pot three-fourths full of water, and bring to a boil over high heat. Add the rice. Reduce the heat to medium and boil gently, stirring a few times, until most of the rice comes to the surface and is tender but slightly firm to the bite. Drain well and rinse.

4 Combine the rice, dried dill weed, lima beans, half of the oil, the turmeric, and salt in a large bowl.

5 Heat the remaining oil in a large saucepan over medium-high heat. Once the oil is heated, arrange the sliced potatoes on the bottom of the pan. Cook for 7 minutes or until the potatoes start to form a crust.

6 Pour the dilled rice over the potatoes to form a nice, even layer. Place a paper towel large enough to cover the surface of the rice. The ends will extend outside the pot. Cover tightly with a lid. Reduce the heat to low and simmer slowly for up to an hour, or until the rice is fully cooked but not mushy. (The towel will absorb the steam, preventing the rice from getting too sticky.) Remove from the heat and let rest for another 30 minutes. The rice will still continue to steam. Gently fluff the rice with a large fork. Mound in a serving dish and serve pieces of the crusty potato bottom on top of the rice.

How to Dry Fresh Dill

1 Preheat the oven to 170°F (77°C).
2 Wash the dill and trim the ends. Pat dry with a paper towel and then spread the dill on a baking sheet in a single layer.
3 Bake in the preheated oven for 2 hours, 30 minutes, or until the dill crumbles off the stem. Discard the stems.

Persian Orange Peel Rice V GF

SHIRIN POLO

At every festive meal in Persian and Afghan homes you will find this sweet, jeweled rice, *shirin polo*, made with basmati rice and perfumed with rose water-infused dried orange peel. It is a dish that is served upside down, from the bottom up; that way, the candied oranges and roasted almonds that have fallen to the bottom during cooking appear at the top. As a child, I remember my mother cutting the orange peel into slivers and then placing the slivered orange peel flat on the table in the breakfast room, to air-dry. To prepare your own peels, refer to the method on the opposite page.

Prep Time: 20 minutes, plus 2 hours for soaking the rice and 30 minutes for the orange peels
Cook Time: 2 hours, plus 4 hours for drying the orange peels
Serves 6

INGREDIENTS

- 2½ cups (575 g) brown basmati rice
- 1 cup (75 g) finely slivered dried orange peel
- 2 cups (500 ml) water
- 1 cup (200 g) sugar
- 1½ tablespoons freshly squeezed lemon juice
- Pinch of saffron threads
- 2 tablespoons rose water
- ¼ teaspoon ground cardamom
- 2 tablespoons salt
- 4 tablespoons oil
- 1 cup (100 g) roasted split blanched almonds (see Oven Roasted Nuts, page 44)

1 Wash and soak the rice according to the instructions on page 32.

2 To make the candied orange peel, place the dried slivered peels into a small saucepan and add enough water to cover. Bring to a boil and boil for 10 minutes. Drain and repeat this step two more times to remove any bitterness. Combine the orange peels, the 2 cups water, sugar, lemon juice, and saffron in the same saucepan and stir over low heat until boiling. Reduce the heat and simmer for about 20 minutes, or until syrupy. Let cool, add the rose water and cardamom and set aside.

3 Bring 9 cups (2 liters) of water to a boil with the salt in a large saucepan. Add the drained rice and boil rapidly for 8 to 10 minutes, or until *al dente*. Drain in a fine-mesh sieve. Pour the rice back into the saucepan and poke 7 deep holes in the surface and drizzle with oil.

4 Place a paper towel large enough to cover the surface of the rice. The ends will extend outside the pot. Cover tightly with a lid. Cook over medium heat, covered, for about 10 minutes, or until steam appears. Reduce the heat to low and simmer for about 30 minutes, or until the rice is tender and the bottom is crisp. (The towel will absorb the steam, preventing the rice from getting too sticky.)

5 Spoon the rice with a flat serving spoon onto a large platter. Break the crust at the bottom of the pot into large pieces and set aside. Top the rice with the candied orange peels and roasted almonds. Garnish with the burnt crust around the top layer to make a decorative and appealing display.

How to Prepare the Orange Peel

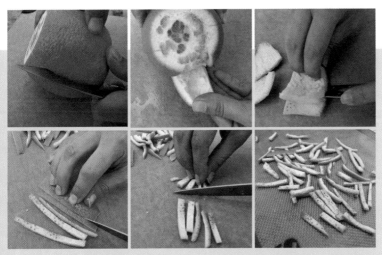

1 You need large oranges with a thick peel and a good small, pointed knife. To sliver the orange peel, cut straight lines down the sides of the orange from the point of the stem to the other end and try to get only the smooth outer layer and as little of the bitter white pith as possible.

2 Peel off the segments without tearing them.

3 Lay the strips with the skin side facing down on a cutting board and sliver away the rest of the pith.

4 Cut the sections into thin matchsticks and then allow them to air dry for four to five days, or until they no longer contain moisture.

5 You can also dry the orange peels by placing them on a non-stick cookie sheet and putting them in the oven at 150°F (65°C). Leave the orange peels in the oven until no moisture is left behind, which will usually take about four hours.

6 Store the dried orange peels in a sealed container, in the fridge. An easier alternative is to purchase ready-made dried orange peels (available in Middle Eastern stores), which you can hold on to for quite a while until you are ready to use them.

Chapter 7
Side Dishes

The produce from your local market can be transformed into an infinite variety of savory side dishes with complex Silk Road-inspired spicing. These dishes appeal to all five senses and promote sustainable eating by using every part of an ingredient, and elevate simple food to the sublime.

As the spices emit their fragrance, you may find yourself taking some long, lingering sniffs that will evoke the essence of the Silk Road region. The spices are so exotic, and they form the perfect union of sweet-spicy-aromatic. Enjoy the seasonal bounty of your local market, and think outside the box with an unfamiliar recipe. You may discover a favorite vegetable you've never tried before.

These vegetable side dishes aren't just about bold flavors, though; sometimes they gently coax diners into submission, working in concert with the main dishes.

Yet, they are a triumph in their own right—do not treat these sides as an afterthought, but an embellishment to the main course. The different elements combine to complement any main dish.

Zucchini with Basil Vinaigrette v GF

As any backyard gardener knows, zucchini is abundant in the United States during the summer months. A low-fat vegetable that is high in vitamin C, zucchini has a delicate flavor that requires little more than quick cooking with olive oil and fresh herbs, such as basil. This recipe originated in Italy—the last country along the Silk Road—where most of my father's side of the family decided to live. Traditionally, the zucchini was fried in olive oil; however, brushing with olive oil works just as well and cuts down on all the grease. Passing this super-easy recipe on to you is my way of saluting *mia familia*.

Prep Time: 15 minutes,
  plus 30 minutes for
  marinade
Cook Time: 15 minutes
Serves 4 to 6

INGREDIENTS

4 tablespoons olive oil
  (divided use)

4 zucchini, trimmed
  and sliced diagonally
  into ¼-in (6-mm)
  oblong pieces

½ cup (15 g) fresh basil
  leaves

2 tablespoons
  balsamic vinegar

1 clove garlic

1 Preheat the broiler and place the zucchini on a broiler rack. Brush the zucchini with 1 tablespoon of the olive oil, and broil 6 in (15 cm) from the heat for 5 minutes, or until lightly browned. Turn the pieces with a spatula and brush with another tablespoon of olive oil. Cook for another 5 minutes, or until lightly browned. Arrange the broiled zucchini on a large platter.

2 Pour remaining olive oil into a food processor; add the basil, balsamic vinegar, and garlic, and pulse until finely chopped. Pour the basil vinaigrette over the zucchini and let it marinate in the refrigerator for at least 30 minutes to absorb the dressing. Serve at room temperature.

Sesame Noodles v GF

I love the nutty, sweet flavor of peanut butter when it's combined with the heat of a hot red pepper. It gives these noodles a snappy flavor. And they're quick to prepare; all of the ingredients are readily available.

Prep Time: 10 minutes
Cook Time: 20 minutes, plus 10 minutes for toasting the sesame seeds
Serves 6 to 8

INGREDIENTS

One 12-oz (350-g) package brown rice spaghetti (available in health food/natural markets)

6 tablespoons chunky peanut butter

4 tablespoons gluten-free or regular soy sauce

3 cloves garlic, minced

1 tablespoon red wine vinegar

1 tablespoon brown sugar

7 tablespoons sesame oil

½ teaspoon red pepper flakes

5 tablespoons toasted sesame seeds (see Toasted Seeds and Spices, page 44), for garnish

3 green onions (scallions) green parts only, thinly sliced, for garnish

2 carrots, cut into thin matchsticks, for garnish

1 Cook the spaghetti according to the package instructions. Once it is cooked, drain and transfer it to a large mixing bowl and set aside.

2 Process the peanut butter, soy sauce, garlic, vinegar, and brown sugar in a food processor for 1 minute. With the motor running, slowly add the sesame oil and red pepper flakes through the feed tube until the mixture is well blended and has a paste-like consistency.

3 Toss the noodles with the peanut butter mixture and 4 tablespoons of the sesame seeds until they are nicely coated.

4 Garnish with thinly sliced green onions, carrots, and the remaining sesame seeds and serve.

Casablanca Quinoa v GF

Prep Time: 20 minutes
Cook Time: 20 minutes
Serves 4 to 6

INGREDIENTS

1 cup (225 g) dried quinoa

3 strands saffron

4 tablespoons chopped dried apricots

4 tablespoons raisins

4 tablespoons sultanas (golden raisins)

2 tablespoons dried cranberries

2 tablespoons shelled pistachio nuts

2 green onions (scallions), green parts only, trimmed and sliced

2 tablespoons finely chopped fresh coriander leaves (cilantro)

2 tablespoons finely chopped fresh mint leaves

Salt, to taste

2 tablespoons extra-virgin olive oil

The replacement of couscous with quinoa does not alter the aromas and flavors of this Moroccan favorite. It's a wonderful variation on the classic, adorned with a medley of colorful dried fruits and nuts.

1 Cook the quinoa according to the package instructions; however, add the saffron to the water.

2 Combine the apricots, raisins, sultanas, cranberries, pistachios, green onions, coriander leaves, and mint in a medium-size bowl.

3 Spoon the cooked quinoa into the dried fruit mixture, season with salt and add the oil and stir to combine. Serve immediately.

Spinach Stuffed Portobello Mushrooms GF

The melt-in-your-mouth filling of savory spinach and feta in this dish is an homage to Greek cuisine. Greek cooking has influenced and been influenced by many other cultures; indeed, it is foremost among "fusion" cuisines, and that can be easily traced back to Alexander the Great himself. Combining modern foods with ancient ingredients is an adventurous journey back in time. Spinach, for example—so essential to Greek cuisine—only became part of its repertoire through the discovery of the Americas. Although these stuffed mushrooms are offered here as a side dish, they could easily be the star of the meal, accompanied by a soup or salad.

Prep Time: 30 minutes
Cook Time: 1 hour
Serves 6

INGREDIENTS

1 large leek, sliced into
¼-in (6-mm) rounds

3 tablespoons olive oil
(divided use)

2 cups (120 g) chopped
fresh spinach or one 10-oz
(330-g) package frozen
chopped spinach, thawed
and squeezed dry

3 cloves garlic, minced
(about 3 teaspoons)

½ cup (70 g) regular or
reduced-fat crumbled
feta cheese

Salt, to taste

Freshly ground black
pepper, to taste

6 portobello mushroom caps

2 Roma (plum) tomatoes,
thinly sliced

2 tablespoons dried
oregano

⅓ cup (30 g) gluten-free
bread crumbs or crushed
unsweetened gluten-free
cereal

1 Preheat the oven to 400°F (200°C).

2 To clean the leek, which absorbs large quantities of sand as it grows, trim off and discard the tough, dark green outer leaves. Slice the leek lengthwise but leave the root intact. Hold it by the root to wash under cold running water. Separate the layers to get all the dirt out. When you are done, cut off and discard the root and slice the leeks.

3 Heat 1 tablespoon of the oil in a large skillet set over medium heat. Add the leek, and sauté for 5 minutes, or until translucent and soft. Stir in the spinach and garlic and cook for 3 minutes, or until the spinach has released its liquid and it evaporates.

4 Remove the spinach mixture from the heat, and stir in the feta until smooth. Season with salt and pepper. Cool for 10 minutes, or until cool enough to handle.

5 Clean the mushrooms with a paper towel. (Never wash mushrooms with water because they absorb it like a sponge.) Place the mushrooms gills-side down in an ovenproof baking dish and bake for 15 minutes.

6 Coat a baking sheet with 1 tablespoon of the olive oil, and place the warmed mushrooms face up on it. Fill each mushroom cap with some of the spinach mixture, and top with a tomato slice. Sprinkle each tomato slice with salt, pepper, and oregano and top each with some breadcrumbs. Drizzle the mushrooms with the remaining olive oil. Bake for 25 to 30 minutes, or until the breadcrumbs are browned and crispy. Serve hot.

Cinnamon-Spiced Butternut Rings V GF

Butternut squash is commonly used in South African cooking, seasoned with cinnamon and curry powder for a nutty, sweet taste. South Africans serve many seasonal side dishes that are rich in both Eastern spices and Western flavors. I have to thank my sister-in-law Janine Solarsh from Johannesburg for sharing this with me across several continents—in true Silk Road style.

Prep Time: 20 minutes
Cook Time: 50 minutes
Serves 6 to 8

INGREDIENTS

⅓ cup (75 ml) olive oil

1 tablespoon brown sugar

2 teaspoons ground cinnamon

4 cloves garlic, smashed

1 teaspoon salt

1 teaspoon curry powder

2 large butternut squash (long, thin ones), peeled and sliced into ¼-in (6-mm) rings

1 Preheat the oven to 425°F (220°C).
2 Whisk together the olive oil, brown sugar, cinnamon, garlic, salt, and curry powder in a mixing bowl.
3 Arrange the squash rings on a baking sheet in a single layer, brush with the spiced oil, and turn and brush the other side. Roast for 40 to 50 minutes, or until golden, crispy and fragrant. Turn with a spatula halfway through roasting.

Maple-Mustard Roasted Parsnips V GF

The parsnip is a root vegetable that is a relative of the carrot; although it is much paler, they do resemble each other. Typically, parsnips form a base in soup, but they can also be roasted for a richer flavor. For this dish, they're caramelized in a maple syrup-mustard mixture and roasted until they take on a deliciously sticky texture, which makes them totally "moreish." You won't be able to resist them.

Prep Time: 15 minutes
Cook Time: 1 hour
Serves 4

INGREDIENTS

2 lbs (1 kg) parsnips, peeled and sliced into 1-in (2.5-cm) medallions

5 tablespoons olive oil

Salt, to taste

6 tablespoons pure maple syrup

2 tablespoons whole-grain mustard

1 Preheat the oven to 375°F (190°C).
2 Put the parsnips into a stockpot and pour in enough water to cover them by 1 in (2.5 cm). Set over medium-high heat and bring to a boil. Drain and transfer them to a baking dish. Toss with the olive oil and season with salt. Roast in the oven for 45 minutes.
3 Meanwhile, mix the maple syrup and mustard together in a bowl. When the parsnips have been in the oven for 45 minutes, pour the mixture over them and toss gently to coat. Roast for another 5 minutes and serve.

Roasted Sweet Potatoes with Coriander Chutney v GF

Here's a fun twist on sweet potatoes; they're spiced with cumin and then dipped in a Coriander Chutney. *Chatni gashneez*, as the chutney is known in Afghanistan, is a tart and tangy condiment for grilled kabobs and rice that is popular on that nation's tables for its lively pungency. When you pair the all-American sweet potato with this Central Asian condiment, you get a delightful fusion of East meets West. You'll need a mortar and pestle for this dish (or a close facsimile), to grind the spices. Some people use a coffee grinder, with good results—as long as it is designated solely for spices or perfectly cleaned of coffee grounds.

Prep Time: 25 minutes
Cook Time: 40 minutes
Serves 6

INGREDIENTS

4 sweet potatoes, cut into
  thin wedges

Spice Paste

4 large cloves garlic, smashed

8 black peppercorns

2 teaspoons salt

2 teaspoons cumin seeds

2 teaspoons coriander seeds

1 teaspoon ground cumin

4 tablespoons sunflower oil

2 teaspoons freshly squeezed
  lemon juice

Coriander Chutney

1 cup (25 g) fresh coriander
  leaves (cilantro)

2 tablespoons crushed walnuts

4 cloves garlic, peeled

4 tablespoons extra-virgin
  olive oil

2 tablespoons freshly
  squeezed lemon juice

1 green Anaheim chili, seeded

Salt, to taste

1 Preheat the oven to 375°F (190°C).

2 To make the spice paste, combine the garlic, peppercorns, salt, cumin seeds, coriander seeds, and ground cumin in a mortar and grind with a pestle as finely as you can. Then add the oil and lemon juice and mix well.

3 Toss the sweet potatoes in the spice paste, making sure they are well coated. Arrange on a baking sheet in a single layer. Bake for 30 to 40 minutes, or until golden and crisp.

4 For the Coriander Chutney, place the coriander leaves, walnuts, garlic, olive oil, lemon juice and chili into a food processor and process until all the ingredients are emulsified. Add a pinch of salt, to taste.

5 Pour the chutney into a small dipping bowl alongside a platter of baked sweet potatoes and dig in!

Lemony Roasted Vegetables v GF

Clear out all the veggies from your fridge for this roasted delight. Although there is a lot of chopping involved here, it is well worth it because there is nothing like a splash of lemon and olive oil with a sprinkling of salt on your freshly roasted veggies to bring the Mediterranean into your house. Serve this with Shawarma-Spiced Potato Wedges (page 164) and turn this side dish into a complete meal.

Prep Time: 25 minutes, plus 30 minutes for eggplant to stand and 30 minutes to marinate
Cook Time: 1 hour, 30 minutes
Serves 6 to 8

INGREDIENTS

1 small eggplant, peeled and chopped

1 tablespoon salt

4 small red potatoes, scrubbed and quartered

2 zucchini, trimmed and sliced into ¼-in (6-mm) rounds

2 tomatoes, chopped

1 red bell pepper, seeded and sliced lengthwise

1 yellow bell pepper, seeded and sliced lengthwise

1 red onion, chopped

2 cloves garlic, minced

Freshly squeezed juice of 2 lemons

3 tablespoons olive oil

Garlic salt, to taste

1 Place the eggplant in a colander and sprinkle 1 tablespoon of salt on it; this will tame any bitterness. Let stand for half an hour, then rinse, drain, and pat dry with paper towels.

2 Place the eggplant, potatoes, zucchini, tomatoes, bell peppers, onion, and garlic into a large roasting pan, drizzle with 2 tablespoons lemon juice and the oil. Season with garlic salt and toss. Marinate, covered, in the refrigerator for 30 minutes.

3 When you are ready to cook, preheat the oven to 350°F (175°C). Place the roasting pan into the oven and roast for 1 hour and 30 minutes. Every half hour, sprinkle some lemon juice and garlic salt onto the vegetables. Toss and return to the oven. Repeat until all the vegetables are well cooked.

Okra Curry V GF
OKRA BHAJI

Native to North Africa, okra was propagated in India in the thirteenth century. Since then, it been a staple in Indian cuisine. This dish is a simple stir-fry of okra with curry spices. Okra can be slimy; to eliminate this, first wash it, pat it dry, and then air-dry it for about 30 minutes.

Prep Time: 20 minutes, plus 30 minutes for okra to dry
Cook Time: 55 minutes
Serves 6

INGREDIENTS

1 lb (500 g) okra

2 tablespoons oil

1 onion, finely chopped

1 Anaheim chili pepper, seeded and minced

1 teaspoon ground cumin

1 teaspoon ground coriander

1 teaspoon ground turmeric

3 tomatoes, peeled and chopped

4 tablespoons water

1 teaspoon salt

Freshly ground black pepper, to taste

Simple Steamed Brown Rice (page 133), or your favorite rice, for serving

Plain yogurt, for serving (optional)

1 Wash the okra, pat it dry and allow it to air-dry for 30 minutes.

2 When you are ready to start cooking, heat the oil in a saucepan set over medium-high heat. Add the onion and sauté, stirring, for 3 minutes.

3 Stir in the chili, cumin, coriander, and turmeric. Continue sautéing for about 8 minutes, or until the onions are translucent and fragrant.

4 Add the okra and stir for a few minutes, or until the okra starts to soften.

5 Stir in the tomatoes, water, and salt and season with a few twists of the pepper mill.

6 Bring the mixture to a boil, lower the heat and simmer, covered, for 30 minutes, or until the okra has released its juices and the tomato has "melted" and formed a thick sauce. Serve hot alongside basmati rice and plain yogurt.

Rutabaga Oven Fries V GF

One perk of belonging to a CSA is that you get to eat foods not normally find in your local supermarket. One example: the rutabaga. This under-appreciated root vegetable has a mild, sweet flavor—with a bit of a bite. Slicing it and tossing it with cinnamon and cumin transforms this pale turnip into a lively, healthful, aromatic alternative to fries.

Prep Time: 10 minutes
Cook Time: 1 hour
Serves 4

INGREDIENTS

4 tablespoons olive oil

1 teaspoon ground cinnamon

1 teaspoon ground cumin

1 teaspoon griyupaprika

4 rutabagas, cut into bite-size chunks

Salt, to taste

1 Preheat the oven to 400°F (200°C).

2 Combine the olive oil with the cinnamon, cumin, and paprika in a bowl.

3 Toss in the rutabaga chunks and coat them in the mixture. Spread out on a baking sheet and roast, turning once, until they're nicely browned, about 1 hour. Toss with salt and serve.

Shawarma-Spiced Potato Wedges V GF

Prep Time: 15 minutes
Cook Time: 1 hour
Serves 6 to 8

INGREDIENTS

12 potatoes, washed, dried and cut into wedges with skin on

4 tablespoons olive oil

4 teaspoons paprika

2 teaspoons Shawarma Spice Mix (page 46, or available in Middle Eastern markets and specialty stores)

3 cloves garlic, minced

Salt, to taste

This is a classic example of foods from two regions meeting up and making friends: potatoes, which originated in the Americas and *shawarma* spice, which comes from the Middle East. Traditionally, *shawarma* are thin slices of meat cooked on a large rotating skewer. Once the meat is cooked, it is sliced off and served with pita—much like a Mexican taco. While the tradition calls for meat, potatoes make a wonderful foil for the spice mixture; the *shawarma* spice gives them a sweet and slightly piquant flavor. When the potatoes are cut into wedges, spiced, and roasted, they make a perfect alternative to ordinary fries; they pack all of the great flavor of spicy fries, but only a portion of the calories and fat. Serve them in a basket lined with pretty napkins to absorb any excess oil, or stand them up in large cups for portable individual servings. They're a fantastic accompaniment to Lemony Roasted Vegetables (page 162), which makes for a light and satisfying meal.

1 Preheat the oven to 350°F (175°C).

2 Spread out the potatoes in a single layer in a large baking dish.

3 Whisk the oil, paprika, Shawarma Spice Mix and garlic in a small bowl.

4 Pour the spice mixture over the potatoes, and toss gently with a wooden spoon, making sure to coat them thoroughly. Season with salt. Bake, uncovered, for 1 hour, or until the potatoes are golden and crispy.

Curried Green Beans V GF

This curried green vegetable dish makes use of ingredients that are very likely locally grown wherever you live, rendering this exotic curry from a faraway land very doable at home. Spiced with fragrant coriander, curry, and ginger, these Indian-style green beans are a great companion to a bowl of steamed basmati rice. Indians tend to like it a bit spicier, oilier, and cooked to the point that we in the United States would consider overcooked. In this version, the green beans are cooked for 30 minutes, but it still tastes close to the authentic Indian dish. Feel free to add or substitute any cubed vegetables of your choice.

Prep Time: 20 minutes
Cook Time: 45 minutes
Serves 6

INGREDIENTS

3 tablespoons oil

1 onion, finely chopped

2 cardamom pods

2 cloves garlic, minced

1 teaspoon minced fresh ginger

1 green Anaheim chili pepper, seeded and minced

1 teaspoon curry powder

1 teaspoon ground coriander

½ teaspoon ground turmeric

½ teaspoon ground cumin

2 lbs (1 kg) green beans, trimmed

3 tomatoes, peeled, seeded and chopped

1 teaspoon salt

Freshly ground black pepper to taste

Simple Steamed Brown Rice (page 133), or your favorite rice, for serving

1 Heat the oil in a large saucepan over medium heat. Add the onion and sauté, stirring and shaking the pan for about 7 minutes, or until translucent.

2 Bruise the cardamom pods: Place the pods on a work surface, place the flat blade of a large chef's knife on top of them and press down on it with the heel of your hand to crush them lightly until the outer husk cracks. Add the bruised pods to the saucepan along with the garlic, ginger, chili, curry powder, coriander, turmeric, and cumin, and sauté, stirring for about 2 minutes, or until fragrant, making sure not to let the spices burn.

3 Add the green beans and tomatoes and season with salt and pepper. Cover and cook over medium-low heat, stirring occasionally, for about 30 minutes. Uncover and cook until the tomatoes have softened into a sauce. Serve with rice.

Chapter 8
Desserts

Along the Silk Road, particularly in Central Asia, it is customary to end a meal with a sweet something—not too sweet though, since their taste buds are used to the sugars of seasonal fruits. A large platter of fresh fruits, compote of preserved fruits, nuts, and *kishmish* (dried fruits) laden the table along with a big pot of chai (green tea) infused with cardamom pods.

Although I was raised in New York, my mother continued the tradition of serving the same desserts she was accustomed to, with the addition of fruity cakes and floral scented cookies. Rather than serve elaborate cakes full of frosting and sugar, typical of Western culture desserts, my mothers' desserts evolved to incorporate both the Silk Road and the West.

I have further elaborated on my mother's desserts and rely on the sugars from fruits for the cakes. For those of you who have a sweet tooth, you may want to modify the sugar content in the ingredient list. The desserts in this chapter are naturally gluten free; using rice and almond flour, which were prevalent in the baked goods along the Silk Road. Unlike the Western baker's pantry, however, the Silk Road's is full of many of the same spices that flavor the savory dishes.

Hamentashen Cookies v GF

The name of these cookies is a reference to Haman, the villain of the holiday of Purim, as described in the Book of Esther. He wanted to abolish Judaism and murder all Jews living in Persia. Traditionally *hamentashen* is eaten every year during Purim to commemorate the victory of the Jews over Haman. These cookies are usually filled with a poppy seed mixture or fruit preserves. Because this is a gluten-free version, it will have a striking pumpernickel color. The batter must be refrigerated for a few hours at least, so be sure to set aside time for that.

Prep Time: 45 minutes, plus 3 hours for the dough to chill
Cook Time: 25 minutes
Makes 20 to 24 filled pastries

INGREDIENTS

⅔ cup (165 g) vegan butter (available in most supermarkets)

½ cup (100 g) packed brown sugar

½ cup (60 g) Applesauce (page 46)

4 tablespoons freshly squeezed orange juice (without pulp)

2 cups (240 g) buckwheat flour

½ cup (60 g) rice flour

2 teaspoons baking powder

1 teaspoon ground cinnamon

¼ teaspoon salt

1 teaspoon pure vanilla extract

One 16-oz (450-g) jar apricot or other preserves

1 Cream the butter and sugar in a medium-size bowl, blending thoroughly, until the sugar is completely absorbed and the butter is light and fluffy. Add the applesauce and orange juice and blend well.

2 Sift 1 cup (120 g) of the buckwheat flour and the rice flour into a large bowl, blending well. Follow by sifting in the remaining buckwheat flour, baking powder, cinnamon, and salt, and add the vanilla. Combine the butter and flour mixtures to form a thick, sticky dough. Cover with plastic wrap and refrigerate overnight, or for least 3 hours, if you're in a hurry.

3 Preheat the oven to 350°F (175°C). Remove the dough from the refrigerator and grease 2 baking sheets.

4 Cut two pieces of waxed paper, about 3 feet (90 cm) long and flour them lightly. Place one piece of waxed paper on a work surface, and place the dough on top. Place the second sheet on top of the dough to form a sandwich. Roll out the dough as thinly as you can, about ¼ in (6 mm) thick, between the sheets of waxed paper. In case you need to roll out the dough a second time, flour both waxed papers again, as the dough is quite sticky to work with.

5 Remove the top sheet of waxed paper slowly, so as not to pull off any dough with it. With a cup or round cookie cutter, cut circles of 3–4 in (7.5–10 cm) into the dough. Drop ¼ teaspoon of filling in the middle of each circle.

6 Roll up the sides to make a triangle, rolling the last corner under the starting point, so that each side has a corner that folds over a corner, and a corner that folds under. This will reduce the likelihood of the filling spilling out.

7 Place the *hamentashen* on the baking sheets and bake for 15 to 20 minutes. Keep an eye on them to make sure the filling does not boil over. Let cool for 30 minutes before transferring them to a wire rack to cool for an hour.

"These cookies are eaten to commemorate a Jewish victory."

How to Form the Hamentashen Cookies

See steps 4–6 in the method for details.

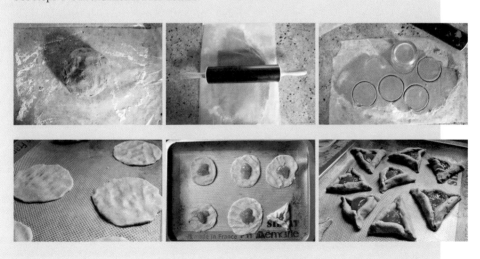

Baked Lemon Rice Pudding v GF

Most rice puddings are cooked in a pot on top of the stove, but this baked version develops into wonderful custard that makes a rich and comforting dessert. Delicately flavored with lemon and a hint of coconut, this dessert can be made anytime with ingredients that are readily available in your kitchen pantry.

Prep Time: 10 minutes, plus 4 hours for soaking the rice, 30 minutes for rice to stand and 1 hour to chill
Cook Time: 2 hours, 30 minutes
Serves 4

INGREDIENTS

½ cup (115 g) short-grain brown rice

2½ cups (625 ml) unsweetened Coconut Milk (page 49)

2 tablespoons packed brown sugar

½ teaspoon pure vanilla extract

Zest of 1 small lemon, grated

1 tablespoon vegan butter (available in most supermarkets), chopped

Fresh strawberries or any seasonal berries, for garnish (optional)

1. Wash and soak the rice according to the instructions on page 32.

2. Combine the rice and coconut milk in a medium-size ovenproof casserole dish and set aside for 30 minutes. This will allow the rice to soften while absorbing the milk.

3. When you are ready to bake, preheat the oven to 300°F (150°C).

4. Add the sugar, vanilla, lemon zest, and butter to the rice mixture and whisk gently to combine. Bake, uncovered, for 2 to 2½ hours, or until the top of the pudding is lightly browned.

5. Allow the pudding to cool, and then gently peel off the skin at the surface and discard.

6. Chill in the refrigerator for about 1 hour, or until the pudding thickens.

7. Garnish with strawberries or any seasonal berries you might prefer and serve.

Peach Cobbler v GF

Plan your summer desserts around the bounty of locally grown peaches. When baked, they morph into sweet buttered heaven. Walnuts add a satisfying crunch. Serve chilled on a hot day with a scoop of vanilla ice cream. If you're out of peaches, try this treat with any summer fruit.

Prep Time: 20 minutes
Cook Time: 40 minutes
Serves 6

INGREDIENTS

4 cups (900 g) fresh peaches, peeled, pitted, and cubed

4 tablespoons packed brown sugar

2 teaspoons freshly squeezed lemon juice

½ teaspoon grated nutmeg

½ cup (50 g) gluten-free rolled oats

3 tablespoons all-purpose gluten-free flour

1 teaspoon lemon zest

¼ cup (½ stick/60 g) vegan butter (available in most supermarkets), chilled and cubed

¾ cup (75 g) walnuts, crushed

1 Preheat the oven to 350°F (175°C).
2 Toss the peaches, 2 tablespoons of the sugar, lemon juice, and nutmeg in a medium-size bowl. Pour into an 8-in (20-cm) pie pan and set aside.
3 Mix the oats, flour, the remaining sugar, and the lemon zest in the same bowl. Add the chilled butter and mix with your hands to form coarse crumbs.
4 Scatter the topping over the peaches and sprinkle with walnuts.
5 Bake for 35–40 minutes, or until bubbling and the topping is golden.

Halvah Parfait v GF

One of the only Israeli dishes to garner world acclaim, this sesame parfait is reinterpreted by chefs in many prestigious restaurants. My version is a creamy vegan dessert that is light and airy. Made with *halvah* (the traditional sesame nougat), a hint of almond and a topping of pistachios and green raisins, it's smooth *and* crunchy—a true Middle Eastern parfait.

Prep Time: 10 minutes
Serves 4

INGREDIENTS

1 package (350 g) silken tofu (soft)

1 cup (200 g) halvah, broken into small pieces

4 tablespoons blanched almonds

1 teaspoon almond extract

1 teaspoon freshly squeezed lemon juice

⅛ teaspoon salt

4 tablespoons crushed pistachios

4 tablespoons green raisins (available in Middle Eastern stores) or sultanas (golden raisins)

1 Combine the tofu, halvah, blanched almonds, almond extract, lemon juice, and salt in a food processor fitted with a metal blade. Process until completely smooth.
2 Spoon into individual dessert glasses and top with pistachios and raisins. Serve cold or store leftovers in the fridge for up to 5 days.

Persian Rice Cookies GF DF

NAAN BERENJI

The faint scent of roses wafted just outside the entrance to my parent's home. When I came home early from elementary school on Friday, my mother would greet me at the door where, inside the house, that same evocative scent perfumed the air and I knew she had baked a traditional dessert: rice cookies scented with rose water and cardamom. Naturally gluten free, this crumbly cookie is dense yet tender, with just the right amount of sweetness. Enjoy this delicate cookie with a bruised cardamom pod in your tea or coffee, if you like. You can bruise the cardamom as my mother did—just bite into it to release the flavor—or crush it with a flat blade. If rice flour is unavailable, grind raw rice to a fine powder in a coffee or spice grinder. Allow time to chill the dough before baking.

Prep Time: 30 minutes, plus 6 hours for the dough to chill
Cook Time: 20 minutes
Makes 20 cookies

INGREDIENTS

1½ cups (325 g) confectioners' sugar

½ cup (125 ml) water

2 tablespoons rose water (available in Middle Eastern and specialty markets)

2¼ cups (270 g) white rice flour

¼ teaspoon baking powder

½ teaspoon ground cardamom

3 egg whites

⅓ cup (75 ml) oil

2 tablespoons poppy seeds or crushed pistachios

1 Combine the sugar and water in a small pot set over medium heat, bring to a boil and stir well for about 5 minutes to dissolve the sugar. Remove from the heat, add the rose water and set aside to cool.

2 Mix the rice flour and baking powder with the cardamom in a bowl. Set aside.

3 Whisk the egg whites with the sugar water in a mixing bowl until soft white peaks form. Add the oil and beat well until fluffy.

4 Gradually fold the beaten egg whites into the dry ingredients with a spatula and mix until thoroughly combined.

5 Place the dough in a container, cover with a plastic wrap and refrigerate for at least 6 hours, but ideally for 24 hours.

6 When you are ready to bake, preheat the oven to 350°F (175°C) and line 2 baking sheets with parchment paper. Take a spoonful of dough about the size of a walnut and roll it into a ball between your palms. Flatten slightly, and place on the baking sheet. Repeat with the rest of the dough, leaving about an 1 in (2.5 cm) between the cookies. (These cookies do not spread when baked.) Sprinkle some ground pistachios or poppy seeds on top of each cookie.

7 Bake for about 15 minutes, or until the cookies are firm and cracked on top. They should still be quite white but have a slightly golden bottom. Remove from the oven and allow to cool before removing them from the waxed paper. Handle gently because these cookies crumble very easily. Store in an airtight container until serving.

Rhubarb Crisp v GF

You know that summer is fast approaching when you see the vibrant color of rhubarb spring up in your local market. When combined with sugar, this red celery-looking stalk transforms into a wonderful, buttery preserve with a tart sweetness that is perfect for this pie. The delectable combination of cinnamon, nutmeg, and vanilla give the rhubarb crisp a heaven-on-earth flavor. If you wish, you can substitute all-purpose gluten-free flour for the oat flour and buckwheat flour. The crisp can be served warm with a nice scoop of vanilla ice cream as a wonderful treat on a hot summer's day.

Prep Time: 30 minutes
Cook Time: 35 minutes
Serves 8

INGREDIENTS

5 stalks rhubarb, cut into ½-in (1.25-cm) slices

½ cup (100 g) packed brown sugar

½ cup (50 g) gluten-free oat flour

½ cup (60 g) buckwheat flour

4 tablespoons almond meal

1 teaspoon baking powder

1 teaspoon tapioca starch

1 teaspoon ground cinnamon

¼ teaspoon grated nutmeg

⅛ teaspoon salt

½ cup (1 stick/125 g) vegan butter (available in most supermarkets)

1 teaspoon pure vanilla extract

¼ teaspoon almond extract

⅓ cup (80 ml) soy milk

1 Preheat the oven to 375°F (190°C). Combine the rhubarb with the sugar in a medium bowl and mix well. Set aside.

2 Whisk together the oat flour, buckwheat flour, almond meal, baking powder, tapioca starch, cinnamon, nutmeg, and salt in another medium-size bowl.

3 Cream the butter, vanilla extract, almond extract, and soy milk in a small bowl until well blended. Pour into the flour mixture and mix until it takes on the consistency of damp, coarse crumbs.

4 Grease a 9-in (23-cm) deep-dish pie pan. Pour the rhubarb mixture into it and top with spoonfuls of the batter. Bake, uncovered, for 35 minutes, or until the top is golden brown and crispy.

Zucchini Loaf V GF

This is the cake I turn to when zucchini season is in full bloom and I have to find creative ways to consume it. It's amazing how this plain-tasting vegetable can transform itself into a delicious cake when loaded with cinnamon, a pinch of nutmeg, and flecked with bittersweet chocolate chips. Although you don't necessarily taste the green squash—and there is a lot of it—it endows this cake with a lip-smacking moistness. I have adapted this recipe from many different sources and fused it into my own gluten-free, vegan version that absolutely does not compromise the taste. It can be stored in the refrigerator for up to a week and freezes really well.

Prep Time: 15 minutes
Cook Time: 1 hour
Makes 2 loaves

INGREDIENTS

- 3 cups (420 g) all-purpose gluten-free flour
- ⅔ cup (130 g) packed brown sugar
- 3 teaspoons tapioca starch
- 2 teaspoons ground cinnamon
- 1½ teaspoons baking powder
- 1 teaspoon salt
- 1 teaspoon baking soda
- ½ teaspoon ground cardamom
- ½ teaspoon grated nutmeg
- 2 large zucchini, cut into thin matchsticks
- ¾ cup (130 g) semi sweet chocolate chips
- ½ cup (60 g) Applesauce (page 46)
- ½ cup (115 ml) oil
- 3 teaspoons pure vanilla extract

1 Preheat the oven to 350°F (175°C). Grease two 4 ½ x 8 ½-in (20 x 10-cm) loaf pans.

2 Sift the flour, sugar, tapioca starch, cinnamon, baking powder, salt, baking soda, cardamom, and nutmeg into a large bowl. Create a well in the center.

3 Add the zucchini, chocolate chips, applesauce, oil, and vanilla extract to the center. Stir until a creamed mixture forms. Pour the batter into the pans.

4 Bake for 1 hour, or until a toothpick inserted in the center comes out clean. Cool in the pans on rack for 20 minutes; then invert the pans to release the breads and cool completely.

Spiced Clove Plum Cake V GF

My parents lived in India for many years as import/export gem dealers before they immigrated to the United States to expand their business. My mother learned this recipe from her Indian employees, who would regularly celebrate Christmas with a plum cake. It is a moist, dense, dark brown cake steeped in a liquefied apricot preserve, which caramelizes at the top to form a splendid crunch. Richly flavored with aromatic spices, this is a dessert that can be eaten all year round. It's great with a chai latte.

Prep Time: 30 minutes
Cook Time: 35 minutes
Serves 8

INGREDIENTS

½ cup (60 g) firmly packed brown sugar

½ cup (1 stick/125 g) vegan butter (available in most supermarkets)

3 eggs, whisked, or 3 teaspoons Ener-G Egg Replacer (available at natural food stores) whisked with 4 tablespoons water

1½ cups (210 g) all-purpose gluten-free flour

1 teaspoon ground cinnamon

¾ teaspoon baking soda

½ teaspoon ground allspice

¼ teaspoon ground cloves

¼ teaspoon salt

4 plums, pitted and sliced

2 tablespoons apricot preserves

4 tablespoons freshly squeezed orange juice

1 Preheat the oven to 375°F (190°C) and grease a 9-in (23-cm) round cake pan.

2 Cream the sugar and butter in a large bowl with an electric mixer set at medium speed until light and fluffy.

3 Pour the eggs or egg replacement mixture into the butter mixture.

4 Whisk the flour, cinnamon, baking soda, allspice, cloves, and salt in another bowl. Add the flour mixture to the butter mixture and beat with the mixer set at medium speed until well blended.

5 Pour the batter into the prepared pan and spread the plums on top in a clockwise pattern.

6 Whisk the apricot preserve and orange juice in a small bowl until the preserve liquefies. Pour it evenly over entire plum cake.

7 Bake for 35 minutes or until a toothpick inserted in the center comes out clean. Let cool for 30 minutes before serving.

Rice-Flour Malabi v GF

Glide your spoon into this lofty white mass and experience the rose-flavored sweetness and a light, creamy texture that will keep you dipping your spoon back until it's all gone. *Malabi* is a Middle Eastern rice porridge that looks like glue until you top it with chopped nuts and a drizzle of syrup. One way to make the rice flour is to process the rice (preferably glutinous) in a food processor—just whirl the rice around until it becomes fine, floury particles—but the resulting dessert will be a bit lumpy. If you prefer a smooth, velvety texture, try to find rice flour in the store, if possible. Although there are variations on *malabi*, my version has a heady, Oriental flavor that comes from the almond extract, rose water with chopped pistachios. If you don't have traditional date honey, a little maple syrup over everything is my American finishing touch to this Middle Eastern sundae.

Prep Time: 15 minutes, plus 1 hour to chill
Cook Time: 20 minutes
Serves 6

INGREDIENTS

2 cups (500 ml) unsweetened Coconut Milk (page 49)

3 cups (750 ml) water

¾ cup (90 g) sweet rice flour

½ cup (60 g) packed brown sugar

2 tablespoons rose water

1 teaspoon almond extract

4 tablespoons chopped pistachios, for garnish

6 teaspoons *silan* (date honey, available in Middle Eastern markets) or pure maple syrup, for serving (optional)

Orange Blossom Date Balls V GF

1 Whisk the coconut milk and water in a medium bowl.

2 Combine ½ cup (125 ml) of the coconut milk mixture with the rice flour in a medium saucepan set over medium-high heat. Stir well to dissolve. Use a whisk to dissolve any lumps, as they are not nice in *malabi*.

3 Slowly whisk in the rest of the coconut milk, plus the sugar, and bring to a boil. Stir well to distribute the rice flour, but don't scrape up the thickened layer that will form at the bottom of the pot; it will simply form undesirable lumps.

4 Lower the heat to medium and cook the pudding, stirring for an additional 5 minutes. Stir in the rose water and almond extract.

5 Let cool a bit before ladling the *malabi* into 6 dessert-size bowls. Cool completely and then refrigerate until it thickens.

6 Before serving, garnish the tops of each with some chopped pistachios and if you wish, a teaspoon of *silan* or maple syrup.

Dates have been a staple food along the Silk Road for thousands of years, with every country along the way transforming them into a tasty delight of its own. They are considered an ideal food packed with nourishing carbohydrates, fiber, naturally occurring sugars, healthy fats, potassium, and B vitamins. You can mix and match different nuts to suit your taste or the contents of your pantry. Complementary citrus, cocoa, and date flavors comprise this delightful, guilt-free confection. Serve cold or refrigerate for up to a month.

Prep Time: 30 minutes
Makes 20 date balls

INGREDIENTS
15 medjool pitted dates
2 cups (200 g) walnuts
¼ teaspoon orange blossom water (available in Middle Eastern markets), plus more for rolling
4 tablespoons shredded coconut
6 tablespoons cocoa

1 Place the dates and walnuts into a food processor fitted with a metal blade and process for about 1 full minute, or until quite smooth.

2 Add the orange blossom water, 2 tablespoons of the shredded flakes, and 4 tablespoons of the cocoa. Process for another 30 to 45 seconds, or until smooth.

3 Once your mixture looks smooth, pour a touch of orange blossom water onto your clean hands (it helps with rolling). Roll ½–1 tablespoon of the date mixture between your palms until you have a nice ball, the size of a walnut. Roll the ball in the remaining coconut and remaining cocoa. Repeat this process with the remaining date mixture. (You don't have to continually put orange blossom water on your hands—just when they feel too sticky to roll a smooth ball.)

Cardamom Banana Bread v GF

This is a variation of banana bread made with cardamom and almond meal, which gives it a welcome twist on the typical banana bread. The buckwheat flour gives this bread a dense yet tender crumb. The almond meal adds a toasted flavor to each slice and crunchy walnuts provide contrasting texture to the soft crumb. The banana bread is naturally sweetened with the ripe bananas, reducing the need for a lot of sugar; the beautiful banana flavor is really all you need. This naturally nutritious bread is perfect with your morning coffee, especially on those hectic mornings when you need to grab something and go.

Prep Time: 25 minutes, plus 1 hour to cool
Cook Time: 50 minutes
Makes 1 loaf (serves 10)

INGREDIENTS

1 cup (120 g) buckwheat flour

½ cup (60 g) sorghum flour

½ cup (60 g) tapioca flour

¾ cup (150 g) packed brown sugar

4 tablespoons almond meal

1½ teaspoons baking soda

1 teaspoon baking powder

1 teaspoon ground cinnamon

½ teaspoon grated nutmeg

½ teaspoon crushed cardamom

1 teaspoon salt

3 ripe mashed bananas

4 tablespoons unsweetened Coconut Milk (page 49)

4 tablespoons oil

2 tablespoons freshly squeezed lemon juice

2 teaspoons pure vanilla extract

½ cup (50 g) crushed walnuts (optional)

1 Preheat the oven to 350°F (175°C). Grease a 4½ x 8½-in (20 x 10-cm) loaf pan.

2 Sift the flours, sugar, almond meal, baking soda, baking powder, cinnamon, nutmeg, cardamom, and salt in a large bowl, and form a well in the center.

3 Mash the bananas in a separate bowl. With a spatula, fold in the coconut milk, vegetable oil, lemon juice, and vanilla. Spoon the banana mixture into the dry ingredients and mix to combine. Add the walnuts, if using.

4 Pour the batter into the baking pan. Bake uncovered for 50 minutes, or until a toothpick inserted into the center comes out clean.

5 Cool for a few minutes before removing from the pan. Invert the banana bread onto a wire rack and let cool completely for at least another hour before serving.

Spiced Carrot Cake v GF

This rich and moist spice cake, full of grated carrots and toasted walnuts, has a warm and grounding flavor. While those pretty orange flecks of slivered carrots give color and texture, they also add sweetness and moisture. An interesting fact about carrots is that they originated in Afghanistan in the purple variety. As carrots moved westward into Europe, the orange variety evolved and the English settlers brought them to America. So when you sit back and enjoy this afternoon treat with a chai latte in hand, pay homage to the Silk Road, for finding its way to America. For an even more decadent flavor, ice the cake with a vegan topping made from raw cashews in lieu of cream cheese frosting.

Prep Time: 30 minutes, plus 30 minutes for mixture to chill, and one hour to cool
Cook Time: 1 hour
Serves 10

INGREDIENTS

⅔ cup (80 g) buckwheat flour

⅔ cup (80 g) brown rice flour

2 tablespoons tapioca flour

¾ cup (150 g) packed brown sugar

1 teaspoon baking powder

1½ teaspoons ground cinnamon

½ teaspoon ground allspice

½ teaspoon ground ginger

½ teaspoon salt

½ teaspoon grated nutmeg

3 tablespoons vegan butter (available in most supermarkets), softened

1 cup (115 g) Applesauce (page 46)

4 carrots, sliced into thin threads

½ cup (50 g) crushed walnuts (optional)

Vegan Cream Icing (optional)

1½ cups (185 g) raw cashew pieces (soaked in water for 6–8 hours and then drained)

⅓ cup (80 ml) water

2 tablespoons agave nectar

1 teaspoon pure vanilla extract

½ cup (60 g) coconut oil, warmed to liquid

1 Sift the flours, sugar, baking powder, cinnamon, allspice, ginger, salt, and nutmeg in a large bowl. Create a well in the center.

2 Fold in the softened butter into the flour mixture. Mix in the carrots, and, if you wish, walnuts. Refrigerate for 30 minutes.

3 Preheat the oven to 350°F (175°C) degrees. Grease a Bundt pan and pour the batter into the pan. Bake uncovered for 1 hour or until a toothpick inserted into the center comes out clean.

4 Let cool in the pan for 15 minutes before inverting onto a rack to fully cool.

5 To make the optional cream icing: Combine the soaked cashews, water, agave nectar, and vanilla extract in a food processor and blend until smooth. Add the coconut oil with the processor running and process until well incorporated, about a minute. Remove the mixture from the food processor, place in a bowl, and chill in the fridge for a few hours until firm enough to spread.

What I especially love about this cookie is that it evolved on the Silk Road and reached the United States in the 1800s. Recipes for almond cookies can be found worldwide; however, their origin can be traced back to the Mediterranean, where Turkey, Spain and Italy all have their slight variations. *Polvorones* are eaten in Spain to celebrate Christmas. In Italy, *ameretti* are enjoyed at any time of the day with tea, coffee, or hot chocolate. A continent away, the Chinese enjoy eating almond cookies with a cup of green tea to celebrate the New Year. I have combined the best of all of these to create a moist, yet crumbly and not-too-sweet cookie that can be served as a special treat to celebrate cultural or religious festivals.

Prep Time: 15 minutes, plus 30 minutes for the dough to chill
Cook Time: 15 minutes
Makes 20 cookies

INGREDIENTS

3½ tablespoons vegan butter (available in most supermarkets)

1¼ cups (175 g) all-purpose gluten-free flour

4 tablespoons confectioners' sugar

Zest of 1 orange

½ cup (60 g) almond meal

2 tablespoons oil

3 tablespoons freshly squeezed orange juice, plus additional juice as needed

1 tablespoon orange blossom water (available in Middle Eastern markets)

¼ teaspoon ground cardamom

⅓ cup (25 g) coarsely chopped almonds, reserving some for garnish

Confectioners' sugar, for garnish

South African Crunchies v GF

This is a variation on a treat that my husband enjoyed as a child in South Africa. They are equivalent to granola bars. However, they are quite firm—perfect for dunking in tea or cocoa.

Prep Time: 30 minutes
Cook Time: 50 minutes
Makes 45–50 crunchies

INGREDIENTS

- 1 cup (2 sticks/250 g) vegan butter (available in most supermarkets)
- 3 tablespoons pure maple syrup
- 1 teaspoon pure vanilla extract
- 2 cups (200 g) gluten-free oat flour
- 2 cups (200 g) gluten-free rolled oats
- 1 cup (75 g) unsweetened coconut flakes
- ¾ cup (90 g) packed brown sugar
- 2 teaspoons tapioca flour
- 1 teaspoon ground cinnamon

1. Melt the butter and pour it into a medium-size bowl. Sift in the flour. Stir in the sugar and rub the orange zest into the dough.
2. Pour in the almond meal and oil, and mix with your fingers until a crumbly mixture begins to form. Add the orange juice, orange blossom water, and ground cardamom and knead into a ball. Cover and refrigerate for 30 minutes.
3. Preheat the oven to 350°F (175°C) and line 2 baking sheets with waxed paper.
4. Remove the dough from the refrigerator and place it on a work surface. Add the coarsely chopped almonds into the dough, kneading it, so that the nuts are distributed throughout. If the dough is too crumbly, add 1 teaspoon orange juice at a time until the dough comes together into a ball.
5. Pinch off a piece of dough about the size of a walnut and roll it into a ball between the palms of your hands. Pat down to flatten; as you do this it will naturally form cracks around the edges. Repeat with the remaining dough.
6. Place the cookies on the baking sheet and garnish the tops with almond flakes. Bake for 15 minutes, or until the base starts to turn a golden brown and the edges are cracked.
7. Remove from oven and cool on a wire rack. Sprinkle with confectioners' sugar.

1. Preheat the oven to 325°F (160°C) and line two baking sheets with waxed paper.
2. Melt the butter in a small saucepan set over low heat. Stir in the maple syrup and vanilla extract until blended. Remove from the heat and set aside.
3. Sift the oat flour into a large mixing bowl and add the oats. Add the coconut, sugar, tapioca flour, and cinnamon. Stir until thoroughly mixed.
4. Make a well in the center of the dry ingredients and add the butter mixture from the saucepan. Whisk all the ingredients together to mix well.
5. Gather the dough with your hands and form it into small balls about the size of a prune. Roll the dough in your hands and then pat each ball down on a baking sheet, about 2 in (5 cm) apart. Bake for 20 to 30 minutes, or until golden brown.
6. Cool on a wire rack until they fully harden, and then store in the fridge or freezer in an airtight container.

Berry-Almond Coconut Scones v GF

Scones, a British import, are made with less sugar and no frosting compared to their muffin counterpart. During the summer months, when blueberries, raspberries, and strawberries fill my CSA box, I like to use them quickly to make a batch of berry scones. Although scones have been around for a couple of centuries, I created a tropical twist to this classic by folding it in with coconut flour, which makes the scones moist, light, and fluffy, with the crunchy texture of almonds. The one-two punch of coconut and almonds in this luxurious scone will make you think you're having your morning coffee under a palm tree. Great for breakfast, an afternoon snack with a cup of tea, or even dessert.

Prep Time: 20 minutes, plus 30 minutes to cool
Cook Time: 15 minutes
Makes 18 muffins

INGREDIENTS

2 cups (200 g) oat flour, or 1 cup (100 g) oat flour and 1 cup (120 g) coconut flour

½ cup (60 g) packed brown sugar

2½ teaspoons baking powder

¼ teaspoon salt

½ cup (1 stick/125 g) cold vegan butter (available in most supermarkets), cut into chunks

1 cup (75 g) sliced roasted almonds (See Oven Roasted Nuts, page 44)

1 cup (100 g) rolled oats

1 tablespoon pure vanilla extract

1 cup (250 ml) cold, full-fat, well-shaken, unsweetened Coconut Milk (page 49), plus extra for brushing

2 cups (200 g) assorted berries

Turbinado sugar, for sprinkling

Indian Spiced Coconut Cardamom Tapioca v GF

1 Preheat the oven to 425°F (220°C) with the rack set at the middle position. Line a muffin pan with paper cups.

2 Combine the oat flour, brown sugar, baking powder, and salt in a large bowl.

3 Cut in the butter with a pastry blender or a knife until the mixture starts to clump into pea-size pieces. Mix in the almonds and rolled oats.

4 Stir the vanilla into the coconut milk in a small bowl. Add the milk to the dough, and stir a few times, be careful not to overmix. The dough should hold together when squeezed, but still be clumpy.

5 Fold in berries until evenly distributed. Pour the batter into the pan. Brush the tops with the coconut milk mixture, and sprinkle with turbinado sugar. Bake for about 15–20 minutes or until golden brown. Do not remove from pan until the scones have firmed up. Continue to cool on a wire rack.

Tapioca pudding stirs up nostalgia for some and distaste for others. Done right, it's one of the lightest, most refreshing chilled desserts. Tapioca is a blank canvas that can be layered with flavor. This particular dessert, with its delicate sweetness spiced with cardamom and ginger, is a perfect ending to an Indian meal. Golden raisins complement this dessert with just a sprinkling on top.

Prep Time: 10 minutes, plus 1 hour for soaking the tapioca pearls
Cook Time: 20 minutes
Serves 4

INGREDIENTS

½ cup (75 g) tapioca pearls

2 cups (500 ml) water

¾ cup (180 ml) unsweetened Coconut Milk (page 49)

2½ tablespoons packed brown sugar

Pinch of saffron threads

¼ teaspoon ground cardamom

¼ teaspoon ground ginger

⅛ teaspoon salt

¼ cup (40 g) sultanas (golden raisins), optional for topping

1 Soak the tapioca pearls in water for 1 hour in a medium-size bowl. (During this time they will soften, enlarge and become a bit translucent.)

2 Whisk together the coconut milk, sugar, saffron, cardamom, ginger, and salt in another medium-size bowl.

3 Pour the tapioca pearls with their soaking water into a medium-size saucepan and bring to a boil. Reduce the heat to medium and stir periodically for 10 to 15 minutes. Stirring the mixture keeps the tapioca from burning or sticking to the pot. The water will become gelatinous and the pearls will become translucent.

4 Pour the coconut milk mixture into the tapioca mixture and stir for an additional 5 minutes. Serve either warm or chilled, optionally topped with a sprinkling of sultanas.

Cinnamon-Apple Cake v GF

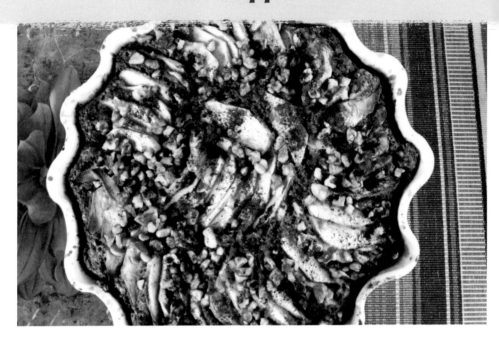

One of the most enjoyable pastimes in the fall is apple picking, and we have ample opportunity in the lovely orchards of Long Island, where I live. When I come home with bags of Mutsu and Empire apples, all I have on my mind is apple cake. This moist, cinnamon-scented apple cake gives off a heavenly aroma, which stirs up so many nostalgic feelings of my home when I was a child. But then, when my fork glides through the light and fluffy cake (perfect for any time of day), I'm back in the delicious here and now.

Prep Time: 25 minutes
Cook Time: 50 minutes
Serves 12

INGREDIENTS

4 apples, peeled and cored

1¼ cups (150 g), plus 1 teaspoon granulated brown sugar

1 cup (120 g) gluten-free oat flour

½ cup (60 g) sorghum flour

½ cup (60 g) tapioca flour

1 teaspoon ground cinnamon

1 teaspoon ground allspice

½ teaspoon grated nutmeg

½ teaspoon baking soda

2 eggs, or 2 teaspoons Ener-G Egg Replacer (available at natural food stores) whisked with 3 tablespoons water

½ cup (115 ml) oil

1 teaspoon pure vanilla extract

¾ cup (75 g) chopped walnuts or pecans

½ teaspoon lemon zest

Indian Rice Pudding V GF

1 Preheat the oven to 350°F (175°C). Grease a 9-in (23-cm) round cake pan.

2 Grate 2 apples or process them in a food processor. Slice the remaining 2 apples thinly and reserve them for use on top of the apple cake.

3 Stir together 1¼ cups (150 g) of the sugar, the flours, cinnamon, allspice, nutmeg, and baking soda in a medium bowl. Make a well in the center.

4 Beat the eggs or egg replacement mixture, oil, and vanilla, and pour into the dry ingredients. Add half the nuts, the grated apples, and the lemon zest. Mix until all of the grated apple is evenly coated. Pour into the pan.

5 Arrange the sliced apples over the cake batter and sprinkle the remaining nuts on top with 1 teaspoon sugar.

6 Bake for 45–50 minutes, or until a toothpick inserted into the center comes out clean. Serve warm or room temperature.

This creamy, filling pudding is scented with a delicate splash of rose water, which fuses beautifully with the saffron and cardamom. The pistachio topping gives it a satisfying crunch, while adding a subtle contrast. It's the perfect dessert for a cool-down after a spicy meal.

Prep Time: 15 minutes, plus 4 hours for soaking the rice
Cook Time: 45 minutes
Serves 4

INGREDIENTS
¾ cup (175 g) short-grain brown rice
1½ cups (375 ml) water
2½ cups (625 ml) unsweetened Coconut Milk (page 49)
3 cardamom pods
½ teaspoon grated nutmeg
Pinch of saffron threads
5 tablespoons packed brown sugar
1 tablespoon rose water
½ cup (50 g) chopped pistachio nuts, for garnish

1 Wash and soak the rice according to the instructions on page 32.

2 Bring the water to a boil in a saucepan and then carefully add the rice. Return to a boil and continue boiling for an additional 15 minutes.

3 Pour the coconut milk over the rice, reduce the heat and simmer, partially covered, for 15 minutes.

4 Bruise the cardamom pods: Place the pods on a flat surface, place the blade of a large chef's knife on top of them and press down on it with the heel of your hand to crush them lightly until the outer husk cracks. Add the bruised cardamom pods, nutmeg, saffron, sugar, and rose water to the rice mixture and cook, stirring occasionally, for 15 minutes, or until the rice is tender.

5 Spoon the rice into small serving bowls, cover, and refrigerate until ready to serve. Right before serving, sprinkle with the nuts.

Acknowledgments

Writing a cookbook is a group effort, and I would like to extend my deepest appreciation to everyone that encouraged me to actualize this book.

Thank you to my smart, savvy, and very patient editor, Karen Berman. I knew when I first spoke to her that she was the perfect match for this book. Karen not only took on the huge job of editing a first-time writer, but she was also enthusiastic about my project. She managed to capture the essence of my ancestry, traveling on a caravan with me through the Silk Road and back to the West. You wore the hat of many people throughout this project: advisor, organizer, and editor. Without your invaluable input and stringing my thoughts together in a fluid way, this project would not have come to fruition.

A very special thank you to P.M. Through you, I found a way to integrate the disparate parts of myself into wholesome and satisfying dishes. It was your encouragement that led me to publish this book professionally.

Thanks to Jennifer Jagusak, who photographed some of my dishes in my home. As much care that I put into cooking my dishes, you took in photographing them to perfection. You can always find her at www.jenniferjagusak.com

My lovely niece Daniella came to my rescue when I needed more photos for this book. You rock, Dani!

Thank you to my family, friends, and community, who all encouraged me to write this book. I was blessed to have many supportive people tell me how important this cookbook is to my Central Asian ancestry. My mother, Zina was instrumental in many of these ancient dishes, always providing her input in how to translate some of these meat dishes into vegetarian. Mom, you are a true artist who has an uncanny ability to make even water taste like champagne. Before sustainability was even in vogue, you always utilized every single part of a fruit or vegetable to make multiple dishes. I am amazed at your creativity and intuition. Your openness to other cultures has transfused itself into my being, my home, and my cooking.

Thank you to my recipe testers and friends; P.M., Alice Merwin, Suzette Diamond, Lea Ruben, and Evelyn Benetar, who also lent me her grandmother's fine china to photograph with some of my dishes.

I am blessed with great in-laws in South Africa. The minute I said I wanted to produce this cookbook, my mother-in-law, Shirley Klein, and sister-in-law, Janine Solarsh sent me countless recipes (written by hand) to experiment with. Your support throughout the process was more than I had ever expected. Thank you for increasing my culinary repertoire.

The Tuttle team did a fabulous job in producing a beautifully rich cookbook that can sit front and center on anyone's coffee table, but hopefully it will sit on the kitchen counter more! Thanks Jon Steever for being my ambassador to the Tuttle team, ensuring that this book met my vision. You all exceeded my expectations.

Last, but not at all least, is my husband, Mervin. You have supported this project of mine and lent me your loving hands for my photography sessions and your stomach for my experimentation.

After reading this manuscript hundreds of times, and wondering to myself how I ever managed to put together a cookbook that looked and sounded so good—I am not a writer, nor a photographer (and quite frankly I am not even a chef!)—I have to thank God who graced me with the words, stamina, and creativity to produce this book.

I welcome your comments on this cookbook or any other queries. You can find me at: **silkroadvegetarian.com**.

Resources of Interest

Preserving Summer's Bounty, by Rodale Food Center and Susan McClure (Editor), Emmaus, PA: Rodale, 1995

So Easy To Preserve, by Elizabeth Anderson and Judy Harrison, Athens, GA: University of Georgia Cooperative Extension Service, 2006

How to Freeze, by Carolyn Humpheries, Slough, UK: Foulsham Publishing, 2003

National Center for Home Preservation
nchfp.uga.edu/how/freeze.html

Ball Preserving Containers (Online Store)
Purchase preserving jars and freezer containers
www.freshpreserving.com

Organizations of Interest

Slow Food USA
Slow Food is an idea, a way of living and a way of eating. The movement links the pleasure of food with a commitment to community and the environment. **www.slowfoodusa.org**

Local Harvest
Find local farmers markets, family farms, CSAs, and other sources of sustainably grown food in your area. **www.localharvest.org**

Spice Resources (with online stores)

Kalustyan's: Fine Specialty Foods
123 Lexington Avenue, New York, NY 10016
Tel: (800) 352-3451 **www.kalustyans.com**

Sadaf: Mediterranean & Middle Eastern Products
Tel: (800) 852-4050 **www.sadaf.com**

Mountain Rose Herbs: Organic Herbs & Spices
Tel: (800) 879-3337
www.mountainroseherbs.com

"Books to Span the East and West"

Tuttle Publishing was founded in 1832 in the small New England town of Rutland, Vermont [USA]. Our core values remain as strong today as they were then—to publish best-in-class books which bring people together one page at a time. In 1948, we established a publishing office in Japan—and Tuttle is now a leader in publishing English-language books about the arts, languages and cultures of Asia. The world has become a much smaller place today and Asia's economic and cultural influence has grown. Yet the need for meaningful dialogue and information about this diverse region has never been greater. Over the past seven decades, Tuttle has published thousands of books on subjects ranging from martial arts and paper crafts to language learning and literature—and our talented authors, illustrators, designers and photographers have won many prestigious awards. We welcome you to explore the wealth of information available on Asia at **www.tuttlepublishing.com**.

Index

A

acorn squash 114
adas polow 146
Afghan Cauliflower Curry 118
Afghan Eggplant Moussaka with
  Garlic Yogurt Sauce 117
Afghan Risotto 140
Afghan Squash Goulash 105
agave nectar 84, 85, 89, 94, 179
all-purpose gluten-free flour 63,
  171, 173, 174, 175
allspice 21, 119, 175, 179, 184
almond extract 171, 173, 176
almond meal 173, 178, 180
almonds 85, 86, 109, 114, 152,
  171, 180, 182
amino acids 34
Anaheim chili pepper 161, 163,
  165
ancho chili pepper 43
anise 23
antioxidants 58, 84, 95
Appetizers 50–65
apple cider vinegar 84
apple juice 36, 47
apples 17, 36, 37, 46, 80, 90, 104,
  109, 114, 122, 124, 144, 184
Applesauce 46, 72, 168, 174, 179
apricot preserves 47, 168, 175
apricots 36, 37, 47
apricots, dried 124, 144, 146, 158
arbol chili pepper 43
arborio rice 32
artichokes 38
ascorbic acid 36
ash-e reshteh 70
Asian Coleslaw 85
asparagus 38
avocadoes 37, 90
Ayurveda 30, 130

B

baby bella mushrooms 89, 109
baby spinach 90, 139
Baked Lemon Rice Pudding 9,
  170
baksh 13, 134, 150
balsamic vinegar 156
bananas 37, 178
barley 34
bases 14, 40, 47, 48, 49, 77, 109,
  160
Bases, Condiments & Other
  Useful Recipes 40–49
Basic Preparation 26–39
basil 156
basmati rice 30, 31, 102, 104–
  106, 108, 111, 112, 116–118,
  126, 132, 133, 135, 136, 138,
  139, 143, 144, 146, 150, 152,
  163, 165
baunjon 65
bay leaves 21, 45, 109
bean sprouts 90
beets 56, 83, 87, 94, 99, 38
bell peppers 55, 95, 119, 162
Bengali Potato & Zucchini Curry
  116
berries 10, 36, 37, 170, 182
Berry-Almond Coconut Scones
  14, 182
bird's-eye chili pepper 77
black grapes 90
black peppercorns 21, 161
black rice 32
blanching 38, 39, 57, 109, 152,
  171
Boiled Rice 33, 133
borani esfanaj 62
borani kudu 105
bouranee baunjan 117
bread crumbs 159
broccoli 24, 38, 88
broth 34, 45, 67, 68, 72, 73, 75,
  76, 80, 104, 105, 111, 114, 118,
  119, 122, 126, 140, 145, 149
brown lentils, dried 28, 68
brown rice 30, 32, 33, 56, 68,
  70, 103–106, 108–112, 114,
  116–119, 122, 124, 126, 129,
  130, 132–134, 136, 139, 149,
  157, 163, 165, 170, 179, 185
brown rice spaghetti 70, 157
brown sugar 46–48, 114, 119,
  157, 160, 168, 170, 171,
  173–176, 178, 179, 181–185
Brussels sprouts 38

buckwheat flour 168, 173, 178,
  179
Bukharian Garlic & Chickpea
  Rice 148
Bukharian Green-Herbed Rice
  134
Bukharian Mung Bean Rice with
  Garlic Oil 130
Bukharian Pilaf with Kidney
  Beans & Carrots 142
Bukharian Slow-Cooked Rice
  with Dried Fruit 144
Bukharian Stuffed Cabbage 122
Bukharian Stuffed Onions 124
Bukharian Tomato Salad 95, 139
Bukharian Vegan Chopped Liver
  52
burgers 48, 110
butter, vegan 114, 168, 170, 171,
  173, 175, 179, 180–182
butternut squash 80, 105, 160
Butternut Squash Soup 80
button mushrooms, white 90,
  119, 134

C

cabbage 24, 38, 42, 85, 95, 122,
  123
calcium 34
carbohydrates 16, 28, 30, 177
Cardamom Banana Bread 178
cardamom pods 21, 136, 138,
  143, 146, 165, 167, 172, 194
cardamom, ground 21, 108, 109,
  111, 143, 152, 172, 174, 178,
  180, 183
Carrot Salad with Garlic &
  Lemon 94
carrots 39, 45, 55, 56, 73–75, 78,
  80, 83, 85, 94, 95, 97, 104, 106,
  107, 114, 122, 124, 138, 140,
  142–144, 149, 157, 160, 179
Casablanca Quinoa 158
cashews 80, 88–90, 138, 179
cassia 22, 23
cauliflower 39, 91, 106, 118
cayenne chili pepper 43, 46, 98
celery 39, 45, 55, 56, 68, 74–76,
  80, 109, 122, 124, 134, 140,
  149, 173
challah bread 65

Chanukah 60
chard 114, 132
chatni gashneez 161
chelow 33, 133, 136, 150
cherries 36, 37
Chickpea Dal in Coconut Broth 111
Chickpea Falafel 54
chickpeas 9, 29, 41, 54, 55, 64, 68, 70, 98, 104, 111, 114, 122, 124, 148, 149
chickpeas, dried 41, 54, 55, 68, 70, 104, 111, 114, 122, 124, 149
chickpeas, skinning 29
chili paste 43, 75, 91, 124
chili pepper 23, 24, 43, 77, 98, 109, 138, 163, 165
chili powder 106–108, 111
chocolate chips 174
Christmas 175, 180
cilantro. *See* coriander leaves
cinnamon stick 46, 146
Cinnamon-Apple Cake 184
Cinnamon-Spiced Butternut Rings 145, 160
cinnamon, ground 20, 22, 23, 46, 68, 72, 81, 103, 104, 109, 111, 112, 114, 119, 122, 138, 143, 160, 163, 168, 173–175, 178, 179, 181, 184
citrus 22, 35, 37, 47, 78, 177
clementines 90
cloves, ground 48, 109, 175
cloves, whole 20–22, 138
cocoa 177
coconut flakes (shredded) 175, 181
coconut flour 182
coconut meat removal 49
Coconut Milk 49, 72, 75, 77, 107, 109, 111, 170, 176, 178, 182, 183, 185
coconut oil 73, 74, 81, 111, 179
coffee 22, 172, 178, 180, 182
Community Supported Agriculture (CSA) 10, 11, 17–19, 42, 61, 72, 83, 88, 163, 182, 187
condiments 40–43, 47, 48
confectioner's sugar 172, 180

containers, for freezing 35
cookies 24, 167–169, 172, 180
cooking beans and chickpeas 28, 29
cooking rice 32, 33, 133, 136
Coriander Chutney 161
coriander leaves 22, 24, 59, 64, 68, 75, 77, 89, 94, 106, 107, 109, 110, 134, 158, 161
coriander seeds 22, 77, 109
coriander, ground 46, 54, 76, 77, 108, 111, 117, 118, 126, 163, 165
corn 10, 34, 39, 138
cranberries 36
cranberries, dried 86, 158
crimini mushrooms 145
Crunchy Broccoli Salad 88
CSA. *See* Community Supported Agriculture
cucumbers 41, 43, 61, 98
cumin seeds 43, 73, 75, 78, 106–108, 111, 138, 146, 161
cumin, ground 43, 46, 52, 54, 65, 74, 76, 89, 91, 103, 104, 109, 111, 114, 116, 120, 122, 126, 134, 140, 149, 161, 163, 165
Curried Green Beans 165
Curried Lentil Burgers 110
Curried Parsnip Soup 81
Curried Spinach Salad with Apples & Grapes 90
curry 43, 76, 104, 107–109, 116, 118, 163, 165
curry powder 22–24, 74, 76, 78, 80, 81, 90, 104, 107, 109, 110, 116, 124, 126, 160, 165

D
daikon radish 94
dairy free 4, 18
dal 78, 107, 111, 130
dal makhani 107
damy 33
date honey 176
Desserts 21, 22, 26, 33, 35, 49, 166–185
Dijon mustard 94
dill 55, 56, 58, 70, 92, 122, 126, 150, 151
dill weed, drying 151

dip 41, 44, 47, 48, 52, 61–63
discoloration, prevention 32, 36, 39
dolma 33, 56, 101, 122
doneness test for rice 33
dry pack 36–38
Duck Sauce 47, 122, 124

E
egg whites 172
eggplant 24, 39, 65, 103, 117, 120, 121, 162
eggs 59, 60, 63, 110, 136, 175, 184
Ener-G Egg Replacer 175, 184

F
falafel 41, 54, 64
fava beans 29
fennel bulbs 86
feta cheese 63, 97, 98, 139, 159
fiber 177
figs 36, 37
flatbread 41
food allergy 26, 30
Fragrant Indian Pilaf 138
freezing food 35, 67, 174, 187
freezing fruit 35, 37
freezing vegetables 38
frittata 58, 62, 92
fritters 54, 63, 110

G
garlic 24, 41, 43, 45, 47, 48, 54, 56, 60–62, 64, 65, 74–78, 84, 87, 89, 91, 94, 95, 99, 102, 104–107, 109–112, 114, 116–120, 122, 130, 138, 139, 143, 148, 149, 156, 157, 159–162, 164, 165
garlic powder 46, 47
ginger 23, 48, 65, 68, 72, 75, 76, 80, 81, 104–110, 116, 118, 119, 132, 138, 165
ginger, ground 24, 80, 81, 114, 116, 144, 179, 183
Gingered Sweet Potato Soup 75
gluten free 4, 30, 33
glutinous rice 32
Golden Earthworm Farm 10, 17, 19

gormeh sabzi 126
goulash 105
Granny Smith apples 46, 114
grape leaves 9, 56
grapes 13, 36, 37, 90
grapeseed oil 54, 60, 63, 65, 110
Greek yogurt 87
green beans 39, 130, 138, 165
green cabbage 85
green chili pepper 65, 98, 138
green herbs 54, 70, 126, 134, 150
green lentils, dried 28, 110
green onions 12, 43, 70, 77, 85, 90, 94, 98, 126, 140, 157, 158
green peas 106, 138
green peppers 77, 117
green raisins 171
green split peas 74, 75
ground red pepper 76, 84, 89, 117, 122
guajillo chili pepper 43
guide to preparing fruit for the freezer 37
guide to preparing vegetables for the freezer 39
gulpi chalaw 118

H
halvah 171
Halvah Parfait 171
Hamentashen Cookies 168, 169
harira 68, 70
harissa 43, 75, 91, 124
honey pack 36, 37
honey syrup 36, 37
hot red chili pepper 43
hot sauce 43, 75
hummus 41, 54
Hummus Dip 41

I
imam bayaldi 120
Indian Red Lentil Falafel 64
Indian Rice Pudding 185
Indian Spiced Coconut Cardamom Tapioca 183
Indian Spinach Curry 108
indigestion relief 21
iron 34, 52, 62
Israeli Chopped Salad 98, 119
Italian Zucchini Fritters 63

J
jalapeño pepper 105, 109
jasmine rice 31

K
kale 84, 114
kateh 33, 133
keftes de prassa 60
khalti 144
khoresh bademjan 102
khoresh ghemeh 112
kibbutzim 98
kitchari 13, 130
kiwis 37
kookoo sabzi 58

L
leeks 39, 58–60, 134, 159
lemon juice 36, 37, 39, 41, 43, 46–48, 55, 56, 68, 78, 87, 91, 92, 94–96, 98, 104, 140, 152, 161, 162, 171, 178
lemon zest 170, 171, 184
lemongrass 24, 77
lemons 60, 68, 96, 122
Lemony Roasted Vegetables 139, 162, 164
Lentil & Carrot Soup 73
Lentil Tomato Soup 68
lentils, dried 76, 78
lettuce 96, 110, 149
licorice 23, 86
lima beans 39, 150
lime juice 77, 89, 94, 99, 107
lime zest 99
limes, dried 112, 126
long-grain rice 30, 32, 33, 132, 136
low-fat 65, 110, 112, 156

M
Main Dishes 101–126
Mango Chutney 48, 63, 65, 110
mangoes 37, 48
maple syrup 72, 160, 176, 181
Maple-Mustard Roasted Parsnips 160
marinade 26, 27, 47, 55, 95, 116, 156, 162
marjoram, dried 44
mast-o-khiar 61

mayonnaise 48, 88, 89
Mediterranean Chickpea Salad 55
medium-grain rice 31
melon 37
mengedarrah 135, 146
meze 41, 51, 55
Middle Eastern Lemon Potato Salad 92
minerals 25, 28, 30
mint 43, 56, 61, 77, 86, 87, 96, 98, 117, 120, 158
mint, dried 70
Minted Beet Salad 42, 87
most laboo 87
mung beans 130
Mushroom Curry 109
Mushroom Wild Rice 97, 145
mushrooms 41, 83, 89, 90, 97, 109, 119, 122, 134, 140, 145, 159
Mushrooms with Cumin 89
mustard 48, 94, 160
mustard seeds 24, 78, 107, 111

N
naan berenji 172
navy beans, dried 70
nectarines 37, 99
North African Chili Paste 43, 75, 91, 124
nougat 171
Nowruz 58, 70
nutmeg, grated 24, 109, 111, 119, 171, 173, 174, 178, 179, 184, 185
nuts 33, 41, 44

O
oat flour 173, 181, 182, 184
okra 39, 163
okra *bhaji* 163
Okra Curry 163
olive oil 41–43, 48, 52, 55, 56, 59, 60, 62, 68, 77, 80, 86, 87, 89, 90–92, 94–99, 103, 105, 112, 114, 117–120, 122, 124, 130, 132, 135, 139, 140, 145, 149, 156, 158–164
one-pot meal 14, 101, 129, 138, 140, 148